JAPANESE ART

Personal Selections from The Mary and Jackson Burke Collection

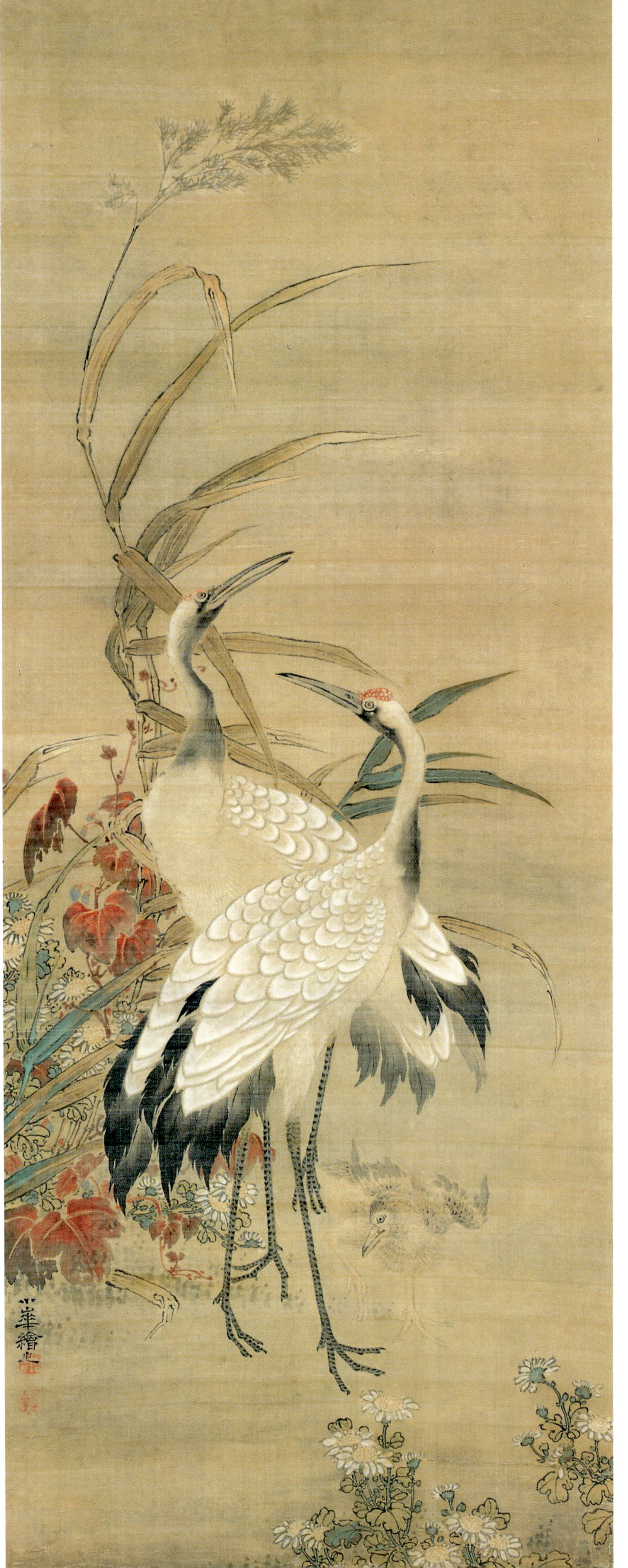

J A P A N E S E   A R T

Personal Selections from The Mary and Jackson Burke Collection

Mary Griggs Burke

The Morikami Museum and Japanese Gardens

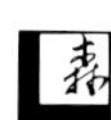

Published on the occasion of the exhibition *Japanese Art: Personal Selections from The Mary and Jackson Burke Collection,* at The Morikami Museum and Japanese Gardens, January 30 through March 28, 1993.

This exhibition and catalogue have been made possible by a generous grant from The Mary Livingston Griggs and Mary Griggs Burke Foundation. The exhibition is also sponsored in part by the Florida Department of State, Division of Cultural Affairs, through the Florida Arts Council. A portion of The Morikami's general operating fund for this fiscal year has been provided through a grant from the Institute of Museum Services, a federal agency that offers general operating support to the nation's museums.

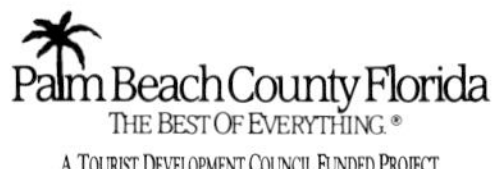

Library of Congress Catalog Card Number 92-085294
ISBN 1-882865-00-6

Edited by Stephanie S. Wada and Georgette Felix
Designed by Tomoko Kawakami Miho
Typeset by U.S. Lithograph typographers, New York
Printed by Offset-litho Jean Genoud, S.A., Lausanne

Printed in Switzerland

Published by The Morikami Museum and Japanese Gardens
4000 Morikami Park Road
Delray Beach, Florida 33446

Distributed in the United States by
The Morikami Museum and Japanese Gardens

Cover:
Scenes from
The Tale of Genji (detail)
six-fold screen; ink, color,
and gold on paper
Edo period, 18th century
153.8 x 358.2 cm

Frontispiece:
Cranes
by Watanabe Shōka (1835–1887)
Signature: Shōka kore o egaku
Seals: Kai-no-in; Shōka
hanging scroll; ink and color on silk
Edo–Meiji period, 19th century
89.6 x 34.5 cm

CONTENTS

FOREWORD

The Morikami Museum is truly honored to present *Japanese Art: Personal Selections from The Mary and Jackson Burke Collection* as the inaugural exhibition of its new galleries. We hoped to open our new museum building with the finest exhibition of Japanese art that could be presented and, if possible, for that exhibition to have some connection with Florida. The Burke Collection emphatically satisfies both criteria.

Having been exhibited in part in several of the major museums in this country as well as abroad, the Burke Collection is widely known as one of the most outstanding private collections of Japanese art. Its Florida connection is genuine. Mr. and Mrs. Burke began collecting Japanese art after seeing the Hart Collection of Ukiyo-e paintings at the Society of the Four Arts in Palm Beach in the early 1960s. Driving down from her Hobe Sound winter home, Mrs. Burke has been a frequent visitor to The Morikami almost since its opening in 1977. She provided the museum with one of its early exhibits, a collection of Nō robe fabrics.

The current exhibition offers a glimpse into the breadth of Mrs. Burke's collecting interests, while unveiling many objects which have not previously been exhibited. Indeed, the selection of objects differs completely from the only previous Florida exhibition of art from the collection, an enthusiastically received show hosted in 1980 by the Orlando Museum of Art (then known as the Loch Haven Art Center).

From objects dating to around the fifteenth century to ceramic works by living artists, the pieces personally selected by Mrs. Burke for the exhibition—from her personal collection and from the collection of The Mary and Jackson Burke Foundation—represent virtually every medium and subject typically found in Japanese art. A number of the best-known artists in the Japanese pantheon are represented, but exquisite works by accomplished masters of lesser renown dominate. These magnificent pieces testify to Mrs. Burke's unerring eye for excellence and refined taste.

Mrs. Burke chose several pieces that display Japanese motifs traditionally associated with an auspicious occasion, befitting the opening of the new museum and emblematic of some of its special interests. Watanabe Shōka's painting of cranes portrays the symbol of the campaign leading to the new museum's construction, as does one of the pair of Raku-ware tea bowls by Ryōnyū. The second bowl depicts tortoises, which abound in Morikami Pond.

The Morikami owes the auspicious nature of this exhibition almost entirely to Mary Griggs Burke, not only for the generous loan of objects from her marvelous collection but for the extraordinary personal effort she has put into every aspect of it. It is not often that we have the opportunity to see and vicariously share in the experience of an outstanding collector's approach to her collection. She has played a most active role not only in selecting the objects but also in deciding how to best display them. In her essay for this catalogue, Mrs. Burke shares with us her connoisseurship and intimate familiarity with the works of art she loves so much.

Our thanks go to The Mary Livingston Griggs and Mary Griggs Burke Foundation, which was instrumental in providing support for the exhibition as well as for the design of the gallery cases. We wish to thank Mr. Marvin Pertzik, Mr. Bayliss Griggs and Ms. Eleanor Briggs of The Mary and Jackson Burke Foundation for their willingness to lend objects belonging to the Foundation. Mr. Pertzik also assisted in making financial arrangements for the exhibit. Additional support for the museum's exhibition program comes from the Florida Department of State, Division of Cultural Affairs, the Institute of Museum Services, and Palm Beach County. Ms. Gratia Williams Nakahashi, Curator of The Mary and Jackson Burke Collection, has provided invaluable advice and assistance in planning all aspects of this exhibition. Mr. Cleo Nichols, designer of both this installation and the permanent exhibition fixtures, brought his vast experience with the Burke Collection and other Japanese exhibitions, his creative eye, and sensitivity to The Morikami's unique characteristics, to create a most pleasing environment in which to experience art.

This project has been of greater magnitude than any in the fifteen-year history of The Morikami. Its rewards, however, are tremendous, for we are hosting an exhibition with a scope and quality never before seen in south Florida. We are proud and exhilarated to be a part of it.

Larry Rosensweig

Director
The Morikami Museum

ACKNOWLEDGEMENTS

It would not have been possible for me to write this catalogue or, for that matter, put together this exhibition of fifty-five objects without the help and advice of my Curator, Gratia Williams Nakahashi. She has done a major share of the basic research, advised me in the selection of objects to be shown at The Morikami Museum, and gracefully dealt with the incredible number of time-consuming details involved in the planning and execution of this exhibition. The success of this enterprise rests upon her shoulders. My Associate Curator, Stephanie Wada, also deserves my gratitude for her invaluable help. She has not only edited my manuscript, she has also completed a variety of important projects connected with the catalogue text, hunted through source materials, and supervised the catalogue photography. There are several others, all friends and experts in the field of Japanese art, who have contributed in many ways to my work on this text. At The Metropolitan Museum of Art, Barbara Brennan Ford, Assistant Curator of Japanese Art, and Masako Watanabe, Curatorial Assistant, supplied some hard-to-find facts on several objects in this exhibition. I would like to thank Mitsuhiro Abe, Master Restorer in the Metropolitan's Department of Asian Art, for assisting in the deciphering of inscriptions and seals, as well as seeing to the conservation needs of the paintings in the exhibition. Shinichi Doi, Assistant Conservator in Objects Conservation, also examined and stabilized a number of the three-dimensional objects. Noelle King O'Connor, Research Assistant in the Department of Asian Art, located source material on Chinese subject matter, and prepared and typed my bibliography. Julia Meech, an independent scholar in Japanese art, also provided me with valuable information from her own research. I am grateful to Fumiko E. Cranston, Research Associate in Asian Art at the Harvard University Art Museums, and Cornelius Chang, scholar of Chinese art, for their translations of poems and inscriptions. Arata Shimao, of the Tokyo National Research Institute of Cultural Properties, kindly sent us the readings of several seals and signatures. Louise Allison Cort, Assistant Curator for Ceramics at the Freer Gallery of Art, gave us her insights on the dating of stoneware ceramics in the exhibition. Miyeko Murase of Columbia University provided me with encouragement to undertake this project, and her many books on the subject of Japanese art served as major sources for my research. I also owe thanks to my secretary, Elizabeth Corbo, who struggled so valiantly with my poor handwriting and bad spelling in typing up the manuscript for publication.

Cleo Nichols, designer of the exhibition installation, worked with Tom Gregersen, Curator of The Morikami, and Larry Rosensweig, Director of the Museum, to realize my dream of displaying these objects in the best possible manner. To them I express my appreciation. My thanks also go to The Morikami's Anne Merrill, Director of Development, and Shoko Y. Brown, Curator of Collections and Exhibitions. I am indebted to Osa Brown, Director of Publications at The Museum of Modern Art, for introducing us to our catalogue designer, Tomoko Miho. Ms. Miho oversaw the progress of this catalogue with sensitivity and a keen eye for detail. Georgette Felix, our editor, helped us to meet deadlines and send this text to press on time. Sheldan Comfert Collins, Carl Nardiello, Otto E. Nelson, and Malcolm Varon provided the handsome photographs. Jack Lucivero, of Marshall Fine Arts, undertook the rigorous task of designing crates and overseeing packing and transportation of the exhibition objects.

I end by thanking the directors of The Mary and Jackson Burke Foundation—Marvin Pertzik, Bayliss Griggs and Eleanor Briggs—for giving me permission to add objects belonging to the Foundation to this exhibition.

Mary Griggs Burke

CHRONOLOGY

Jōmon period	10,500–400 BC
Yayoi period	400 BC–AD 250
Kofun period	AD 250–600
Asuka period	AD 600–710
Nara period	AD 710–794
Heian period	AD 794–1185
Kamakura period	AD 1185–1333
Nambokuchō period	AD 1333–1392
Muromachi period	AD 1392–1573
Momoyama period	AD 1573–1615
Edo period	AD 1615–1868
Meiji period	AD 1868–1912
Taishō period	AD 1912–1926
Shōwa period	AD 1926–1989
Heisei period	AD 1989–

JAPANESE ART

Personal Selections from The Mary and Jackson Burke Collection

Mary Griggs Burke

As I am an inveterate collector, I have enjoyed the process of selecting works of art from The Mary and Jackson Burke Collection and Foundation for an exhibition to mark the opening of The Morikami Museum's new building. After examining objects gathered over three and a half decades of collecting and ranging in date from about 2500 B.C. to the early twentieth century, I chose pieces which not only appeal to my taste but offer a picture of the wide range of materials represented in the collection. In order to create an exhibition which is cohesive yet rich in variety, I selected objects which date, for the most part, to the Edo period (1615–1868). Earlier pieces include three paintings dating to the Muromachi (1392–1573) or Momoyama (1573–1615) periods; among the later paintings is a pair which dates to the Meiji period (1868–1912). One large lacquer box is a nineteenth-century object; five ceramics and two lacquer pieces were produced during the second half of the twentieth century. These later works are characterized by a fresh approach to execution, but they are still traditional enough in feeling to be viewed in the context of the Edo period.

The Edo era (named after the city of Edo, or present-day Tokyo) was an extremely innovative and productive time in the arts of Japan. Early traditions were rejuvenated, further developed or transformed. In spite of strict edicts by the Tokugawa regime, which forbade the Japanese to travel abroad, outside cultural influences did eventually filter through the isolationism imposed by the shogunate to enrich the stylistic vocabulary of painters and craftsmen. This exhibition contains examples of nearly all of the major schools of Japanese painting that evolved over the centuries and continued to function during the Edo period. The major concern of the exhibit is not, however, one of scholarly matters or the chronological arrangement of works of art. I have, instead, placed an emphasis upon enjoyment: first, my pleasure in the kind of art I have collected, and, of equal importance, what I think might please and amuse its viewers. The majority of these pieces have not been recently shown in this country; many have never been exhibited. Yet they are fine objects that have, in the past, been overlooked in favor of better-known but not necessarily better examples of Japanese art.

Perhaps the most compelling consideration for the inclusion of an object in this exhibition was whether or not it could be shown to advantage in the galleries of the newly created Morikami Museum building. This criterion is not as frivolous as it may seem. What made the invitation to lend objects from The Mary and Jackson Burke Foundation and my private collection attractive to me, and to the trustees of the Foundation, was the idea that this new building represents one of the first American attempts to create a museum based on Japanese design for the purpose of presenting Japanese culture to the public.

To be properly appreciated, Japanese art depends (more than the art of other cultures) on being shown, if not exactly in context, at least in surroundings that take into account the aesthetics of the country of origin. This does not imply that Japanese art is inferior to or weaker than the art of other cultures. In past eras, when these treasures were first created, the Japanese displayed them in a carefully designed environment of simple, natural elegance. A beautifully crafted object in lacquer, wood, or metal and an elegantly mounted hanging scroll of calligraphy or painting were usually placed, with a simple flower arrangement, in the *tokonoma*, an alcove created for this purpose. The alcove functioned as an integral part of a room; the walls were constructed of earth or wood of a natural color, while the floors were covered with *tatami*—modular mats of fragrant rushes. These natural textures complemented the two or three carefully chosen objects in the *tokonoma* and with them formed a spare but pleasing composition—simple and peaceful.

The late Jun'ichirō Tanizaki (1886–1965), one of Japan's best-known novelists, gives an insight into the way in which past generations of cultivated Japanese viewed art objects in a *tokonoma*. He writes:

> The Japanese room does have its picture alcove, and in it the scroll and the flowers serve not as ornament but rather give depth to the shadows. We value a scroll above all for the way it blends with the walls of the alcove, and thus we consider the mounting quite as important as the calligraphy or painting. Even the greatest masterpiece will lose its worth as a scroll if it fails to blend with the alcove, while a work of no particular distinction may blend beautifully with the room and set off to unexpected advantage both itself and its surroundings. Wherein lies the power of an otherwise ordinary work to produce such an effect? Most often the paper, the ink, the fabric of the mounting will possess a certain look of antiquity and this look... will strike just the right balance with the darkness of the alcove and the room.
>
> Jun'ichirō Tanizaki, *In Praise of Shadows*, 1977, p. 19

For Tanizaki, the combination of the old painting with the flower arrangement in a dark alcove produced a sense of absolute harmony. The room containing the *tokonoma* existed, in turn, as a functional unit in a well-proportioned house. The house was traditionally situated in its own small garden, which had been as painstakingly designed as the architecture of the building. Ideally, a distant view beyond the fence—"borrowed" scenery—completed the ensemble.

It would of course be impossible to re-create the shadowed beauty of the kind of interior that Tanizaki describes in such nostalgic terms. Even if it were possible, such a house could not be used as a modern museum. An art object today cannot be presented as it would have been at the time of its production. There are matters of preservation and safety to be considered, and the need to make it available for public appreciation, rather than the delectation of a few connoisseurs and their friends. An effective museum display must, therefore, be the result of compromise. The gallery of The Morikami Museum has been planned specifically for the showing of Japanese art, and an architectural enframement has been created in the Japanese taste. Much has been achieved through suggestion; simplicity and neutral colors are stressed, crowding is avoided, and attention has been paid to proportion and balance. Cleo Nichols, the designer, has created a most successful display area, which has made the choosing of objects a pleasure.

I believe that it is possible to appreciate most of the works of art in this exhibition without knowing where they fit into the history of Japanese art. However, knowledge of a certain amount of background material does help one to appreciate and enjoy them further. In this small catalogue, the best that can be done is to present a few general facts with illustrations from the material at hand. For anyone who is deeply interested in Japanese art, I suggest further reading of books and articles cited in the bibliography. This is essential to flesh out the incomplete and therefore simplistic picture I present in these pages.

In considering the character of Japanese art it becomes clear that two major trends dominate its history from at least the sixth century on. These are, first, the Japanese dependence on cultural influence

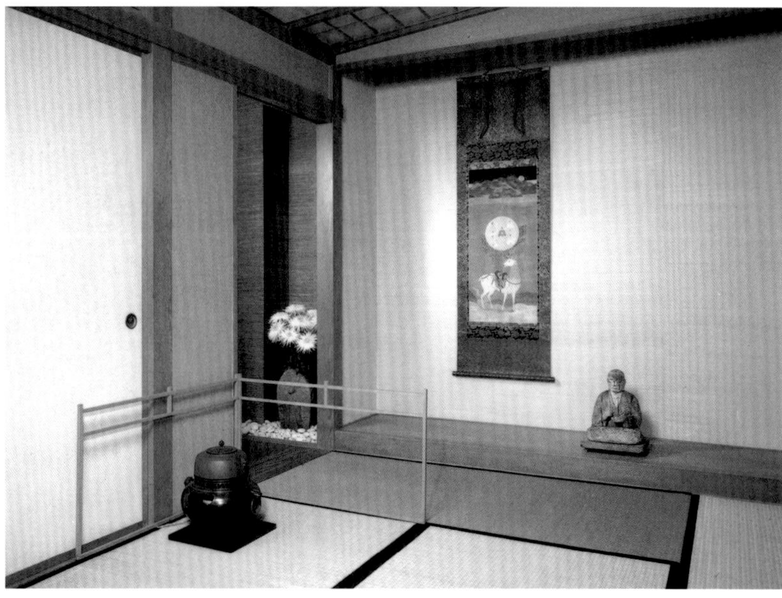

Interior of tea room
Residence of
Mary Griggs Burke
New York

from the Asian continent—especially China—and, second, the development and strengthening of an indigenous Japanese aesthetic.

The Japanese have an incredible ability to borrow from other cultures and adapt what they have taken to suit their own needs and taste. Cultural impact from mainland Asia helped to shape the direction of Japanese art and arrived in three major waves. In the sixth century Buddhism was introduced from China via the kingdoms of Korea. In the thirteenth century Zen Buddhism brought the concept and technique of ink monochrome painting. Finally, during the Edo period, Chinese printed books and literati-style paintings entered Japan.

A fourth influence came during the sixteenth and early seventeenth centuries, from the Western nations of Spain, Portugal, Holland, and England. The temporary presence of these foreign traders had two effects upon Japanese artists: some made delightful depictions of the *namban* (southern barbarians) and their ships on screens and other objects, while others copied the style of European paintings. After most foreigners were banned from entering the country in the seventeenth century, the Dutch, allowed only into Nagasaki, served as a tentative conduit for foreign culture for the duration of the Edo period. It was not until the Meiji period that the full impact of Western influence was felt by the Japanese.

Religious Thought and Imagery

Japan's native religion of Shinto was a loose body of beliefs and myths devised in ancient times by an agricultural clan society to explain the natural processes—such as seasonal change—which might result in a good harvest. All natural phenomena held great significance for these people, and the worship of local divinities grew up around certain striking features of the countryside, such as lakes, streams, mountains, or forests. Eventually a single clan, claiming descent from the sun goddess, gained control over the others, and these ancient myths and practices became the beliefs and rituals of Shinto. Polytheistic Shinto saw nature as the manifestation of divine presence, and the Shinto pantheon of deities is overwhelming, consisting of *kami*—spirits or gods—which pervade all aspects of life and nature. *Kami* overlook human activities and dwell in man-made objects as well; others are deified ancestors and great figures from the past.

Buddhism arrived in Japan in the mid-500s, and its impact on Japanese culture was profound. The Buddhist sects that first arrived in Japan were chiefly those of the Mahayana, or "Greater Vehicle." Mahayana stressed the achievement of salvation through the worship of deities, dedicated to protect the nation and its rulers, who provided believers with material as well as spiritual blessings. From this core of belief came the offshoots of Esoteric and Pure Land Buddhism and Zen.

Esoteric Buddhism *(Mikkyō)*, which utilizes ritual and secret initiations, enabled the Japanese to reconcile their native Shinto gods with Buddhist deities, facilitating a peaceful coexistence of the two religious traditions. Indigenous *kami* became identified with Buddhist gods, and Shinto shrines and Buddhist temples often existed within the same compound. Since Shinto lacked a tradition of pictorializing its deities, the first Shinto icons were influenced by Buddhist sculptures and paintings. A sculpture of Sōgyō Hachiman (or Hachiman in the guise of a Buddhist monk, Fig. 1/No. 29) and a portrait of the monk Rigen Daishi (Fig. 2/No. 1) are interesting examples of Shinto and Esoteric Buddhist imagery. The latter work will be discussed first, as the subject is a monk, albeit a distinguished one, whose depiction is not complicated by the blending of Buddhism and Shinto that we find in the figure of Sōgyō Hachiman.

Rigen Daishi (832–909), also known as Shōbō, was a monk of Shingon Buddhism (an Esoteric sect), who founded the temple of Daigoji, southeast of Kyoto, during the 870s. I was delighted to acquire this portrait, as it reminded me of a wonderful experience I had in 1980, when I and friends visited a subtemple of Kongōbuji on beautiful Mount Kōya, south of Osaka. This temple was established by the celebrated monk Kūkai (774–835, posthumously known as Kōbō Daishi), who introduced Shingon to Japan early in the Heian period (794–1185).

We ascended the mountain in early April on a slowly moving train. A light sprinkling of snow covered the pine trees on the gradually rising slopes of the mountain and its foothills. The vistas around us seemed to unroll like an ink-landscape handscroll. The subtemple in which we stayed is a beautiful old building constructed over a mountain stream. It is part of a monastic compound whose garden is graced with a thirteenth-century pagoda and provides a quiet retreat for monks as well as visiting pilgrims like ourselves. Awakened in the early morning by a resonant gong, we watched the mysterious rituals, encircled by awe-inspiring, richly adorned esoteric icons with many arms and heads.

In this painting from the Muromachi period, Rigen Daishi is depicted holding a *vajra*, an Indian implement symbolizing the power of Buddhism to penetrate the darkness of ignorance. In his other hand he holds the tip of his robe. These features form the standard iconography for his portraits, of which a number of earlier examples exist in both painting and sculpture. This is an imaginary portrait, executed long after Rigen Daishi's death, and is thus an idealized and impersonal vision of the man. The inscription above the figure reads:

Wisdom
All things are formed by the mind
Wisdom's path which is spoken of
comes entirely from quietude.
Trans. Cornelius Chang

The sculpture of Sōgyō Hachiman, while of uncertain date, is carved in the style of the twelfth century. This deity holds a jewel in his left hand and may have grasped a monk's staff with his right. He may have once been brightly colored. Such a work is an example of the Japanese effort to reconcile their native religion with the powerful forces of imported Buddhism. Hachiman is generally identified as the Shinto god of war, but he was one of the first Shinto deities to be assimilated into Buddhism. Here, his shaved head and monk's robe testify to the belief that Shinto gods had to become monks in order to seek Buddhist enlightenment and become bodhisattvas. Because of the figure's monastic garb, it is difficult to distinguish the image from a portrait sculpture of a real monk, although true monk portraits tend to be more realistic, stressing individual characteristics.

Many different types of Shinto painting developed during the

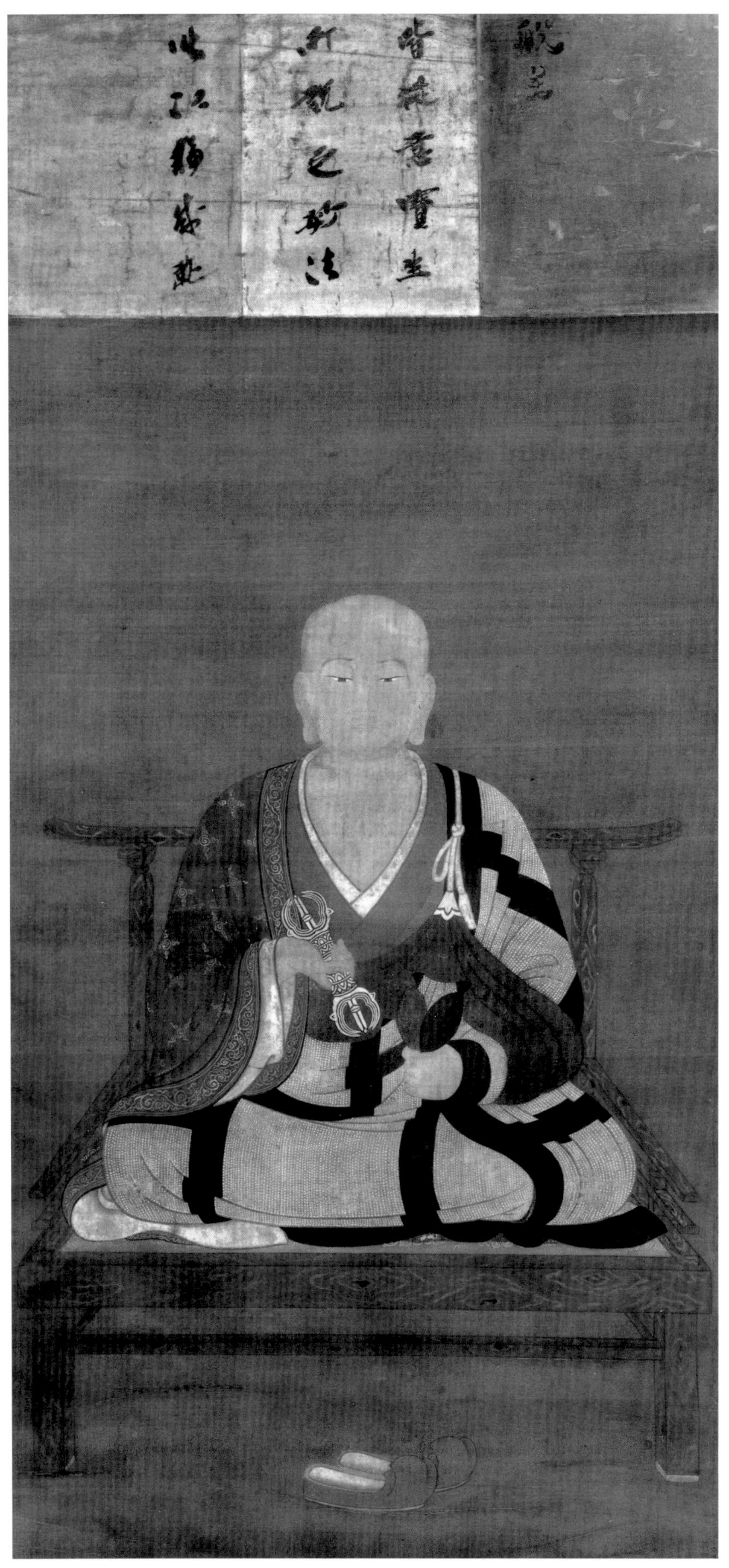

Fig. 2 / No. 1
Portrait of Rigen Daishi
hanging scroll; color and ink on silk
Muromachi period, 16th century
90.5 x 41.9 cm

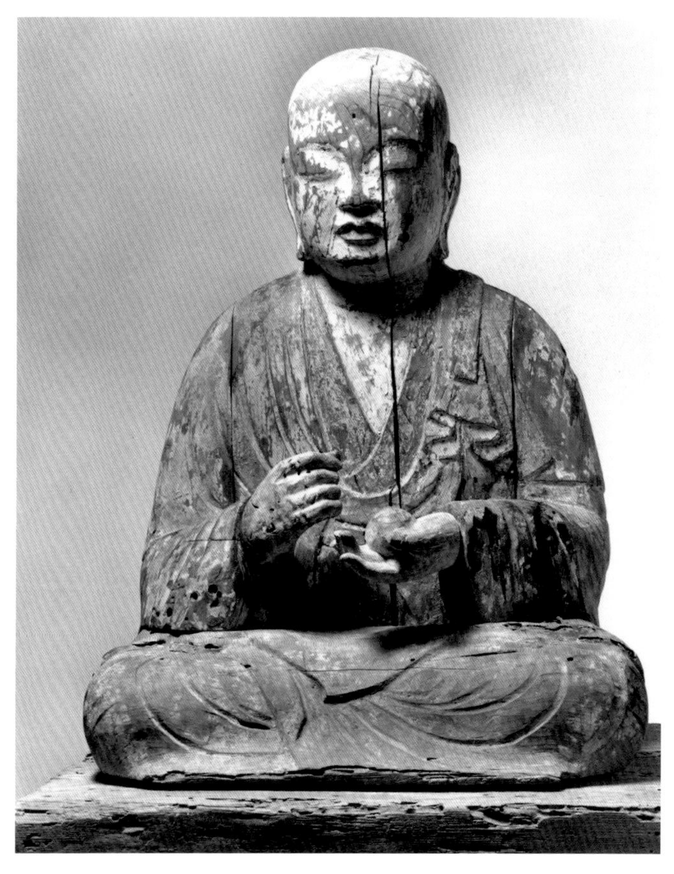

Fig. 1/No. 29
Sōgyō Hachiman
wood with traces of pigment
Heian period, 12th century(?)
H: 34.3 cm

later Heian period. Their wide thematic range included depictions of *kami* individually or in groups and with or without corresponding Buddhist deities. Maplike representations of shrines, votive plaques, narrative scrolls, and "dream visions" of *kami* also abounded. Many Shinto paintings are designated as *mandala*, a term borrowed from Buddhism to refer to pictorial arrangements of divinities which indicate their interrelationships and respective places in the universe. In certain instances, Shinto shrines and their surroundings become the subject of *mandala* painting. Festival and pilgrimage *mandala* focus on human activity. In contrast to these images, other *mandala* illustrate a single figure or motif, such as a deity astride a deer, or even a deer alone.

The *Kasuga Deer Mandala* (Plate 1/No. 2) in this exhibition is of the latter type of Shinto painting, and it may be dated to sometime between the late Muromachi and early Edo periods. Many shrines in Japan are associated with sacred animals, which are regarded as vehicles or messengers of the *kami*. At the Kasuga shrine in Nara, it is the deer that is sacred, and even today herds of deer roam freely through the sacred compound. This *Deer Mandala* depicts a white deer with a branch of *sakaki* ("sacred tree") upright on its decorated saddle. On the *sakaki*, which symbolizes the presence of the god Takemikazuchi no Mikoto, rests a disk, or sacred mirror with images of the five principal Kasuga deities in court costume. The origins of the Kasuga cult can be found in local worship of agricultural deities who were believed to inhabit Mounts Mikasa and Kasuga; in this painting, with its charming, freely executed rendition of the landscape, the rounded mountains are touched with autumn colors. This handling of pictorial elements recalls the native classical approach to landscape painting, which expresses the essence of Japanese scenery.

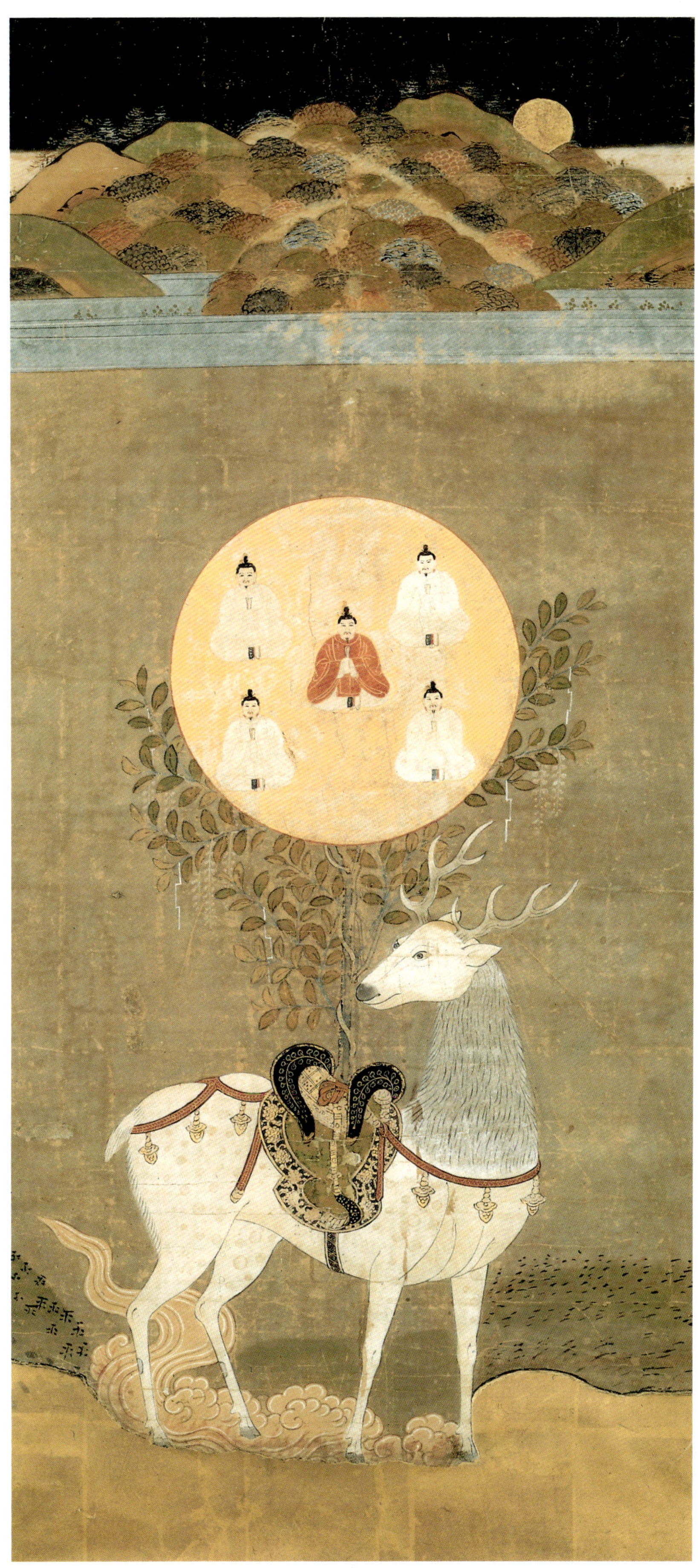

Plate 1 / No. 2
Kasuga Deer Mandala
hanging scroll; color and
ink on paper
late Muromachi period to early
Edo period, 16th–17th century
89.9 x 40.0 cm

Native Literary Themes in the Arts

When Buddhism came to Japan from mainland Asia, it brought with it the high culture of China. Even more importantly, it gave the Japanese the means to express their own language in writing. Having no written language of their own, they adopted the character system used by the Chinese. As the Chinese and Japanese languages are extremely different in grammatical structure, sound, and inflection, the Japanese finally developed their own *kana* script, a syllabary of approximately fifty abbreviated symbols derived from Chinese characters. Ultimately, Japanese came to be written in a combination of Chinese characters (*kanji*, in Japanese) and native *kana*. From an aesthetic viewpoint, the juxtaposition of complex characters with simple, delicate *kana* was highly appealing, while use of *kanji* promoted a cultural bond among the Chinese, Japanese, and Koreans.

Written Chinese continued to be used for official purposes for many years. During the late Heian period the Japanese employed the new *kana* script for a greater freedom of expression in their own language. The use of *kana* facilitated the growth of a vernacular literature, which paralleled the development of a native approach to narrative illustration, the colorful *yamato-e* (literally, "Japanese painting").

Yamato-e represents the first flowering of Japanese decorative style. The word itself is a reference to the heartland of Japan, the region around the present-day cities of Nara and Kyoto; the suffix *e* means "picture," or "painting." The term is used generally to describe the mainly secular paintings that differed in style from paintings produced under Chinese influence. Landscapes painted in the *yamato-e* manner emphasize seasonal change, and subjects are often places made famous by poems and other works of literature.

By the late Heian period the Chinese-influenced culture of the seventh through ninth century had been replaced by a uniquely Japanese culture centered around the court and the sophisticated aristocracy. These all-powerful nobles devoted their lives to pleasure and beauty, and they controlled not only the affairs of state but all decisions concerning standards in literature and the arts. All aspects of the highly refined (if hedonistic) court culture conformed to an aesthetic pattern that included the use of the beautiful *kana* script for the composition of narrative and verse. The aristocrat's life of splendor and luxury is best described in *The Tale of Genji* (*Genji Monogatari*), the masterpiece of Japanese classical literature written in the eleventh century by the court lady Murasaki Shikibu.

As interest in China waned, courtiers increasingly turned to the cultivation of the native thirty-one-syllable *waka* poem. Indeed, the art of poetry was more a part of the world of the Heian courtier than that of any other society in history. Poetry competitions were held, lovers exchanged poems, and, on occasion, officials even communicated through verse. Inability to compose a *waka* or failure to recognize a poetic allusion could condemn one to social disgrace.

To demonstrate the Heian-period obsession for composing poetry and illustrating it with *yamato-e*, I chose one of the most exquisite and feminine works in the Burke Collection. It is an album of miniature paintings, depicting thirty-six court poetesses. The paintings and their accompanying poems are mounted on silk cut in the shape of fans. The poems, one above each figure, are inscribed in elegant calligraphy. The tiny, jewel-like portraits were executed during the seventeenth century in a manner reminiscent of the much earlier Heian period. They reflect aspects of the painting style adopted by the courtly Tosa school of artists in the beginning of the fifteenth century, and Tosa painters continued to work in this mode until the end of the nineteenth. The typical Tosa style was characterized by delicate line, meticulous attention to detail, lavish use of color, and decorative compositions. Tosa artists specialized in courtly themes and scenes from classical literature.

This album illustrates several important points concerning Heian literature in general and poetry in particular. While poetry was written by almost every person of status, men used the Chinese language more frequently than women. Women were actually discouraged from such pretensions to scholarship. They therefore appear to have taken full advantage of *kana* script and are credited with initiating the fashionable pastime of the poetry contest. Records indicate that both judges and contestants in the earliest contests were women, although their roles were later taken over by men.

Women clearly played a seminal role in the development of *waka*; however, when the first selection of *kasen*, or "Immortal Poets," was made in the eleventh century, few female poets were included in the group. Most popular listings of *waka* masters consist of thirty-six poets, with Kakinomoto no Hitomaro (active late seventh to early eighth century) in the premier position. This album is a late example of an imaginary poetry contest devoted entirely to women. The poetesses are dressed in the rich, multi-layered garb of rainbow hues favored by Heian court ladies, and the long, sinuous strands of their black hair create delicate patterns against the colorful robes. The faces are doll-like, devoid of expression or individuality. Rank is indicated by the "curtains of state" and *tatami*–mat platforms provided for princesses. The poetesses illustrated here are identified as Lady Ise (ca. 877–940), on the left (Fig. 3/No. 20), and Princess Shikishi Naishinno (1153–1202), on the right (Plate 2/ No. 20). The poem which represents Ise reads:

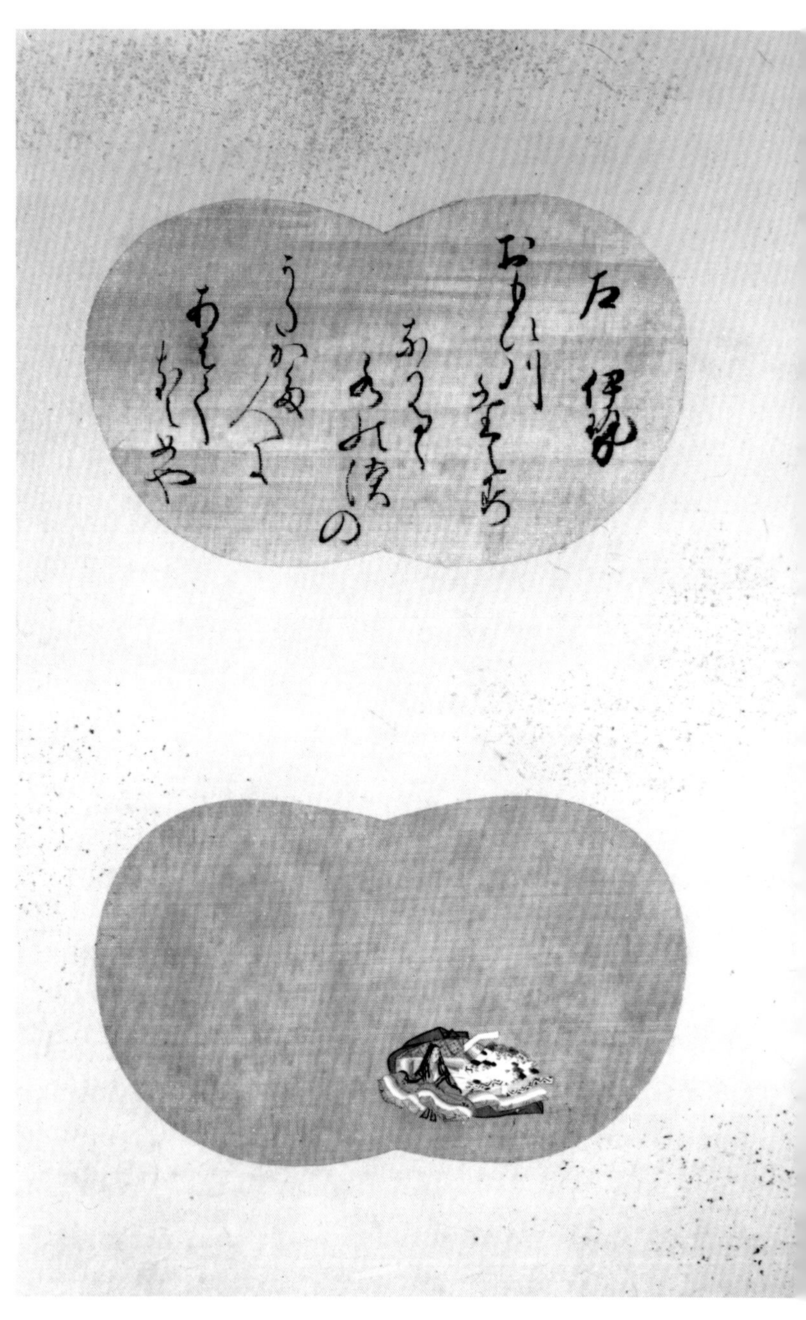

Fig. 3 / No. 20
Thirty-six Immortal Poetesses
album with 36 leaves;
ink, color, and gold on silk
Edo period, 17th century
Ptg. 6.1 x 9.8 cm (each leaf)
Call. 6.3 x 10.1 cm (each leaf)

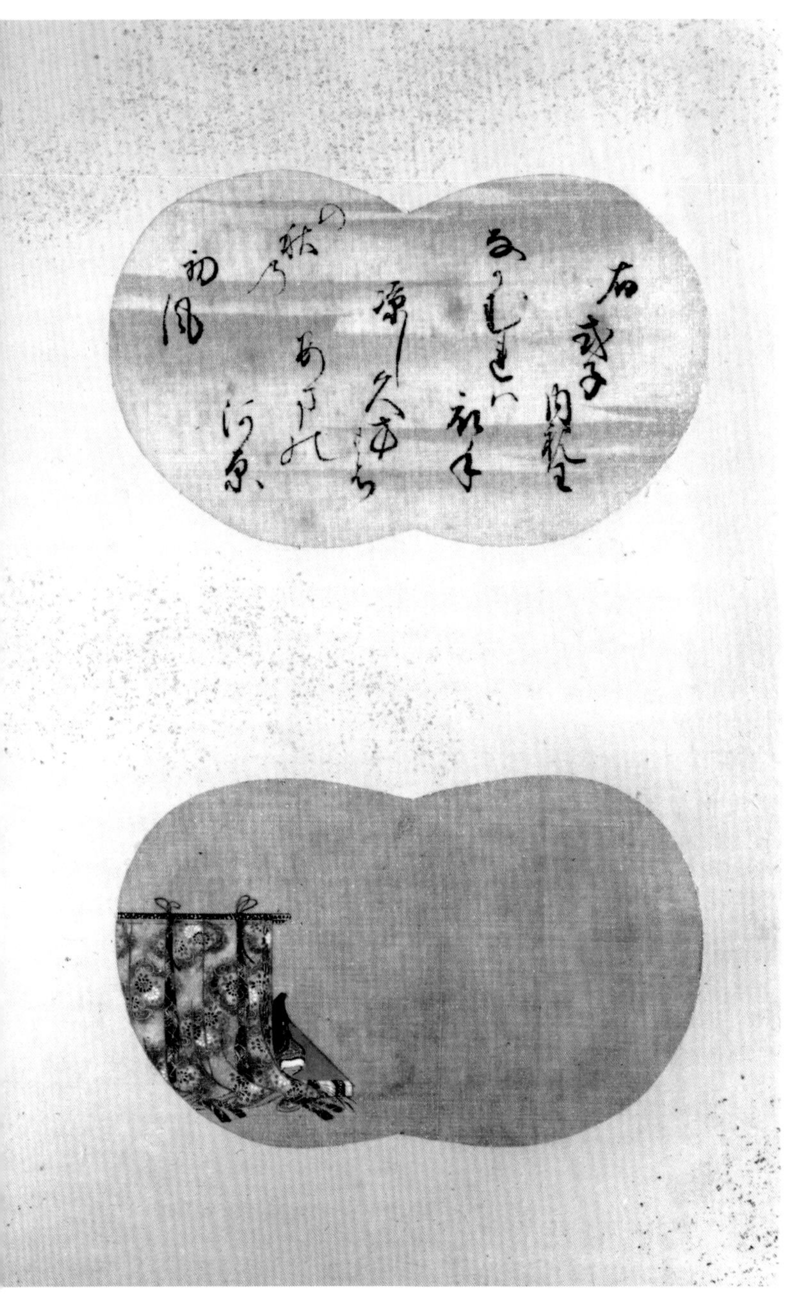

Omoigawa	The River of longing
Taezu nagaruru	flows on, never stopping.
Mizu no awa no	The froth on the water
Utakata hito ni	meets no one
Awa de kiemeya.	and dies away as ephemeral bubbles.
	Miyeko Murase, *Tales of Japan*, 1986, p. 64

Ise was a descendant of the Fujiwara line, and her name derives from the province in which her father, Fujiwara no Tsugukage, served as governor. Her beauty and grace were greatly admired and she became romantically involved with a number of high-ranking courtiers. Emperor Uda (r. 887–897) was the father of her first child; years later, she gave birth to a daughter, Nakatsukasa, who became one of the "Thirty-six Immortal Poets."

Shikishi's poem may be translated as follows:

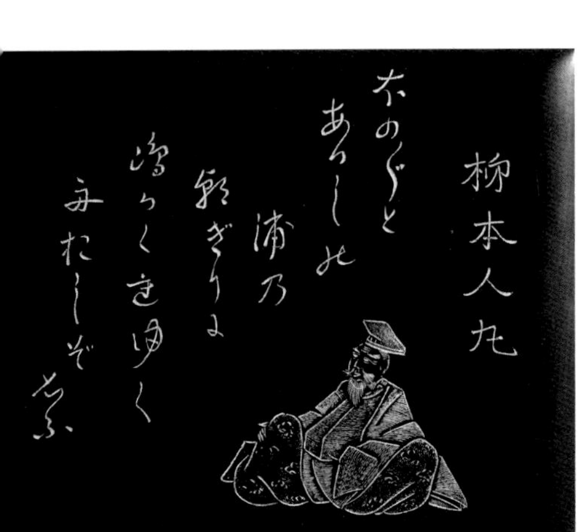

Nagamureba	When I gaze at
Koromode suzushi	the Milky Way,
Hisakata no	My sleeves become
Ama no kawara no	cooled by
Aki no hatsukaze.	Early autumn wind.
	Trans. Fumiko E. Cranston

According to Fumiko E. Cranston, the melancholy verse is a reference to the myth of two stars, the Herdsman (Altair) and the Weaving Maid (Vega), lovers who are allowed to meet only one night out of the year.

Shikishi was the daughter of Emperor Goshirakawa (r. 1155–1158), and as a child she served as ceremonial priestess of the Kamo Shrine in Kyoto. She studied under the greatest poet of her day, Fujiwara no Shunzei (1114–1204); in later life, suspected of plotting against the government, she took Buddhist orders.

The "Immortal Poets" are also depicted on the nineteenth-century set of stacked lacquer boxes (Fig. 4/No. 52) in this exhibition. The poets, outlined in gold and accompanied by their poems, decorate the sides of the boxes. Their most revered representative, Hitomaro, is featured on the lid (Fig. 5/No. 52). As in most of his extant "portraits," he is depicted with a wispy beard and lined face; he also wears a courtier's cap. His well-known verse reads:

Honobono to	Dimly, dimly
Akashi no ura no	In the morning mist that dawns
Asagiri no	Over Akashi Bay,
Shima gakure yuku	My longings follow with the ship
Fune o shizo	That vanishes behind the
omou.	distant isle.
	Miyeko Murase, *Tales of Japan*, 1986, p. 72

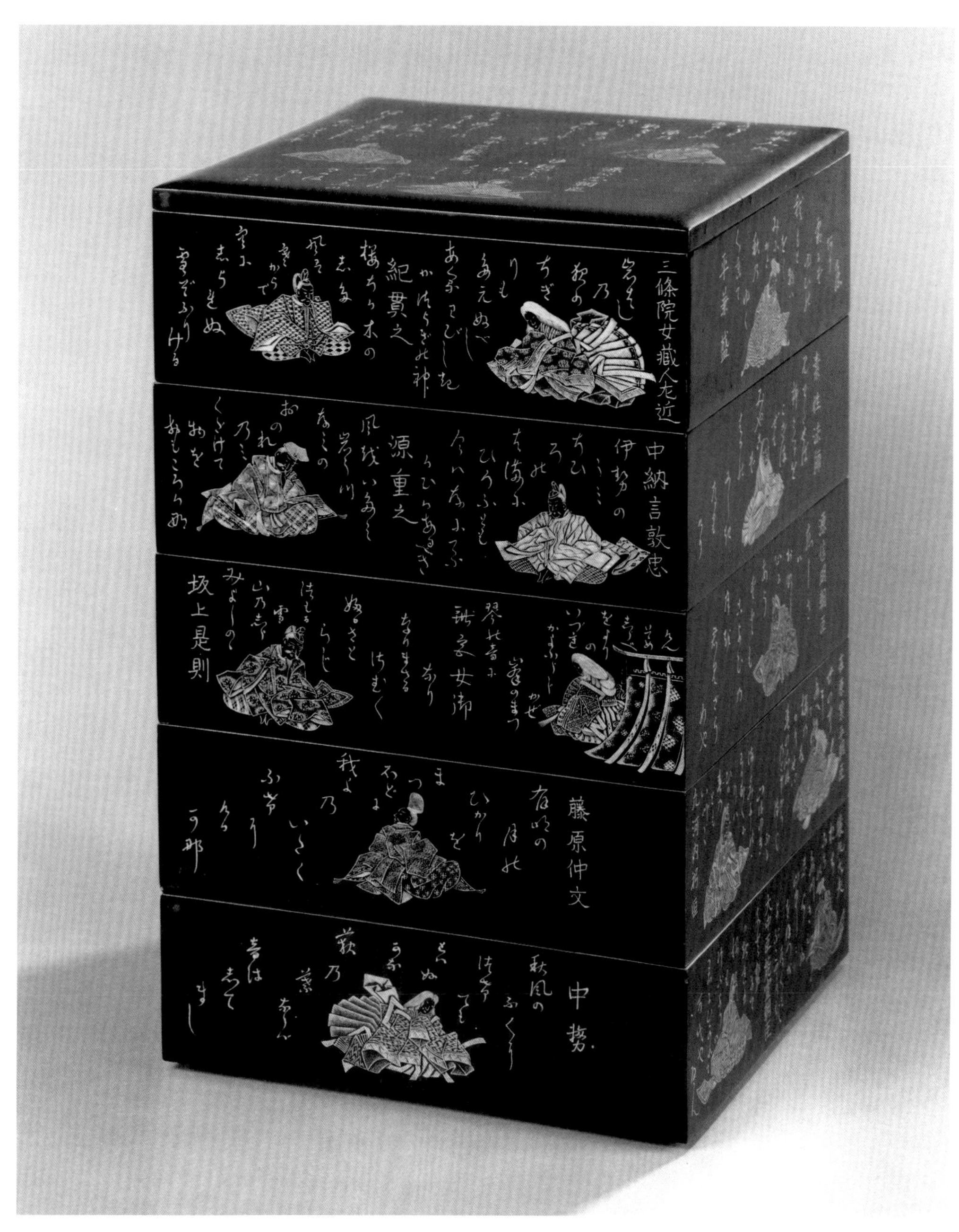

Fig. 4, Fig. 5 (detail) / No. 52
Stacked boxes with design of the
Thirty-six Immortal Poets
black lacquer
incised and colored with gold
19th century
H: 45 cm, L: 25.9 cm, W: 24.4 cm

As noted above, Heian-period court life was best described in *The Tale of Genji*, undoubtedly the most famous work of Japanese literature. The narrative, regarded by many as the world's first true novel, follows the life of the fictional Prince Genji, a man of high birth, great beauty and intellect, and a compassionate lover of women and nature. The first forty chapters of this monumental fifty-four-chapter novel are devoted to his amorous adventures. The remaining chapters focus on the less spectacular achievements of his son and grandson. Between the time in which it was written and the present day, the *Genji* has been illustrated by innumerable artists in every conceivable format of painting. The earliest extant illustrated version of the tale dates to the early twelfth century and is a supreme example of *yamato-e*. Sherman Lee explains this type of painting very clearly, as follows:

> The compositional devices depend upon the use of all the available space from the bottom to the top edges of the scroll. Horizon lines are almost non-existent for the painters wished to decorate the entire surface, even suggesting movements beyond the horizontal boundaries of the paper. Arbitrarily placed cloud bands... are used inside as well as outside of rooms as boundaries or ties between adjacent areas. Architecture is treated most arbitrarily. The roofs of houses are removed to permit a partial bird's eye view of the interiors. Diagonals of screens, shutters, walls, mats or flooring create... patterns and directional movement.
> Sherman Lee, *Japanese Decorative Style*, 1961, pp. 28–29

In *yamato-e*, use of pattern is of the greatest importance, from treatment of the larger architectural framework to the most detailed textile designs. Figures, conforming to their decorative environment, are heavily draped in patterned materials, with simplified, completely idealized faces. It has been suggested that in early *Genji* illustrations the emotional tenor of each scene is indicated by compositional arrangement rather than movement or expression on the part of the characters.

The colorful, Edo-period *Genji* screen (Plate 3/No. 26) in this exhibition owes much of its decorative character and basic composition to the famous early *Genji* paintings. This work has a special significance for me, as it was the first important work of Japanese art that I acquired. It was purchased at auction in 1956, when I knew little or nothing about Japanese art except that it had great appeal for me. I had visited Japan the year before to study Japanese gardens, with a view to installing one near my new house. When I saw the screen in New York, I thought how wonderful it would be to have it as a decoration in my home. I was not aware of its fragility, nor of the importance of having a pair of screens as opposed to a single screen; therefore, I purchased only one and let its mate go to another bidder. Much later, I traced the mate to Frank Lloyd Wright's Taliesin in Spring Green, Wisconsin.

This screen puts together scenes from six *Genji* chapters to form a most pleasing arrangement of pictorial motifs. An episode from Chapter One, "The Paulownia Court," occupies the first three panels (from right to left) at the top of the screen. It depicts Genji's coming-of-age ceremony; at the age of twelve, he receives the cap of an adult and his hair is ritually cut. The scene found at the bottom of the first panel from the right is taken from Chapter Three, "The Shell of the Locust." It shows Genji peeking through a partially opened screen at a provincial governor's wife with whom he has become enamored. The third scene, at the top of the fourth panel from the right, is from Chapter Five, "Lavender." Here Genji sees Murasaki, the girl who later becomes his favorite wife, for the first time. The seventeen-year-old prince, accompanied by his retainer, peers over a wattle fence. Murasaki, still a child, is attended by her ladies, nurse, and young companions; they are watching her pet sparrow, which can be seen flying away.

The fourth episode fills up the bottom of the two central panels. This splendid scene from Chapter Seven, "An Autumn Excursion," depicts the culmination of a royal trip to the Suzaku Palace, with musicians, dancers, and courtiers. The giant drums on the left, balanced by red leaves on the right, are particularly decorative. Genji and his friend To no Chūjō dance in the center space.

The fifth scene, from Chapter Fourteen, "Channel Buoys," occupies the top of panels five and six. While in exile, Genji has had an affair with a lady of Akashi. She bears him a daughter, who is eventually married off to the future emperor. This illustration shows Genji and his entourage resting after a lengthy trip to Naniwa (near present-day Osaka). Genji's retainer, Koremitsu, brings him a brush and ink so that he may write a note to the Akashi lady, whose boat has entered Naniwa Bay.

The sixth and final scene, in the lower left-hand corner of the screen, represents Chapter Twenty-three, "The First Warbler." It is the New Year, and the child of the Akashi lady is now a young girl. Genji and Murasaki are visiting her; they watch young page girls and serving women picking seedling pines for New Year's decorations. The Akashi lady has sent her daughter New Year's delicacies in a "bearded basket."

Another popular method for illustrating *The Tale of Genji* appears in an album of twenty leaves, attributed to the Tosa school. At one time, the paintings in this album were probably interspersed with pages of abbreviated text in *kana* script. The two scenes displayed here represent Chapter Four, "Evening Faces" (Fig. 6/No. 22), and Chapter Twenty-five, "Fireflies." In Chapter Four, Genji passes a house with an attractive vine of "evening faces" *(yūgao)* flowers growing on a trellis. His curiosity is aroused as he glimpses several

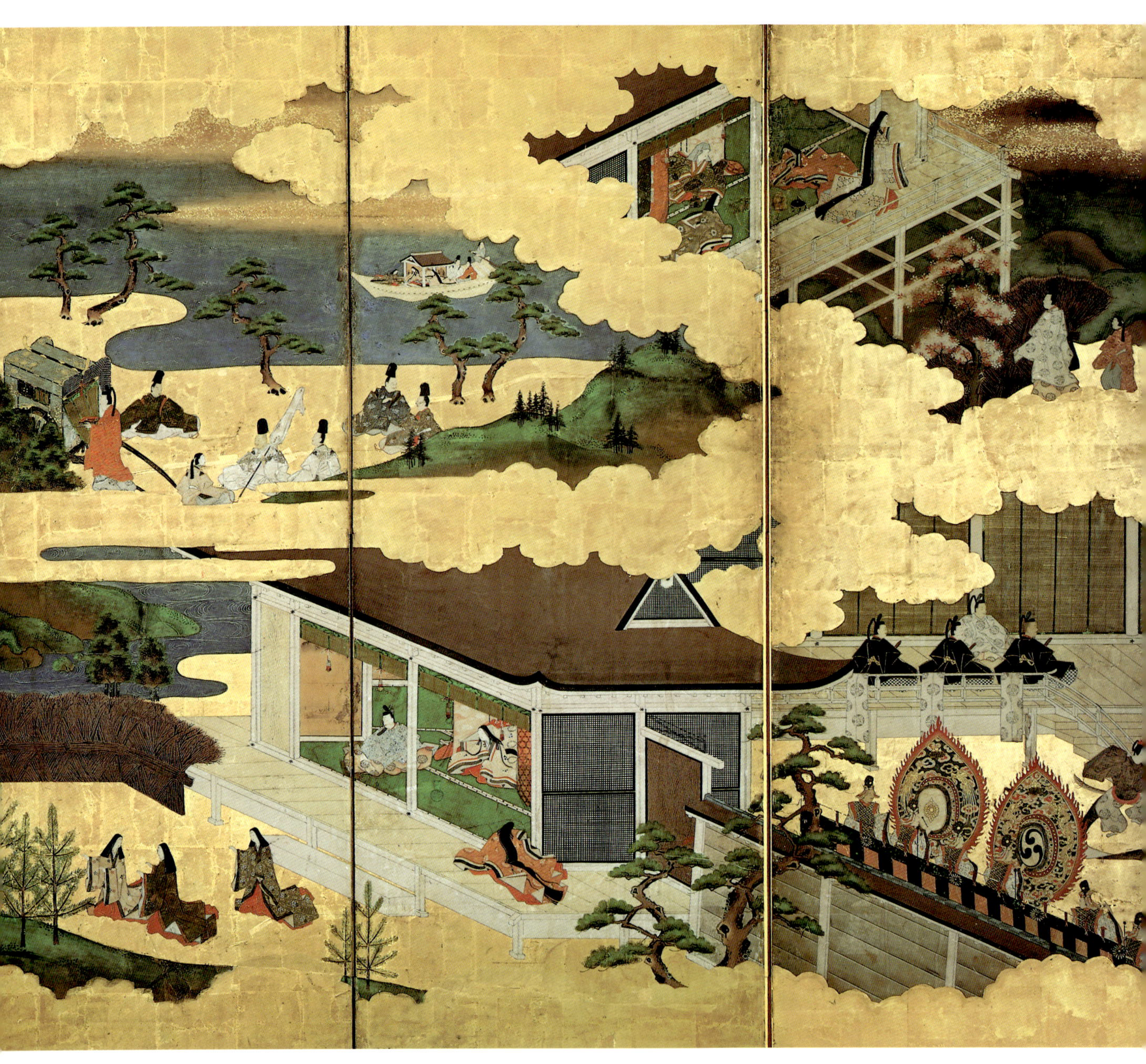

Plate 3 / No. 26
Scenes from *The Tale of Genji*
six-fold screen;
ink, color, and gold on paper
Edo period, 18th century
153.8 x 358.2 cm

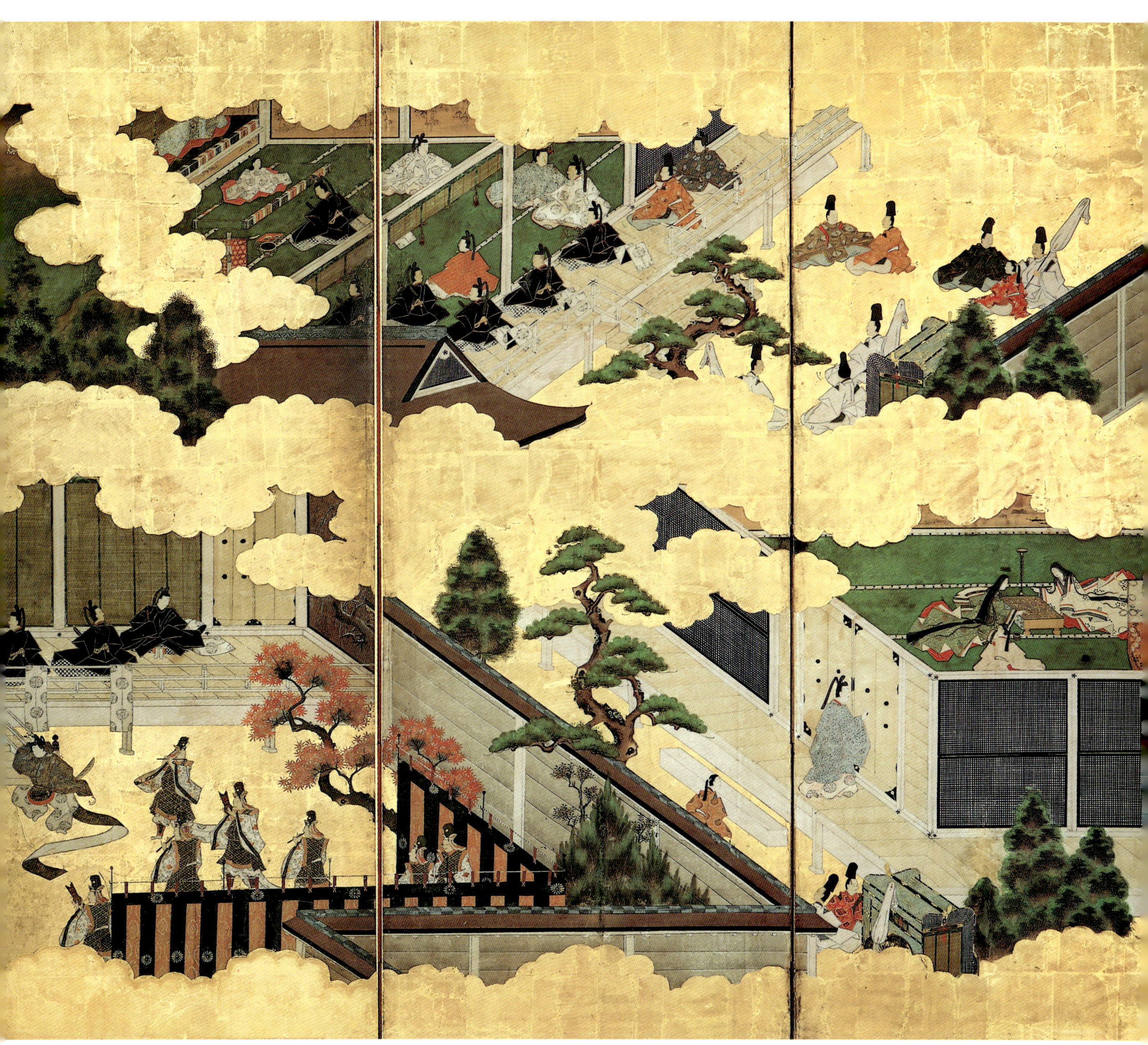

Fig. 7 (detail) / No. 19
"Aoi" episode from
Chapter 9 of *The Tale of Genji*
handscroll; ink on paper
Muromachi period, 16th century
12.0 x 572.0 cm

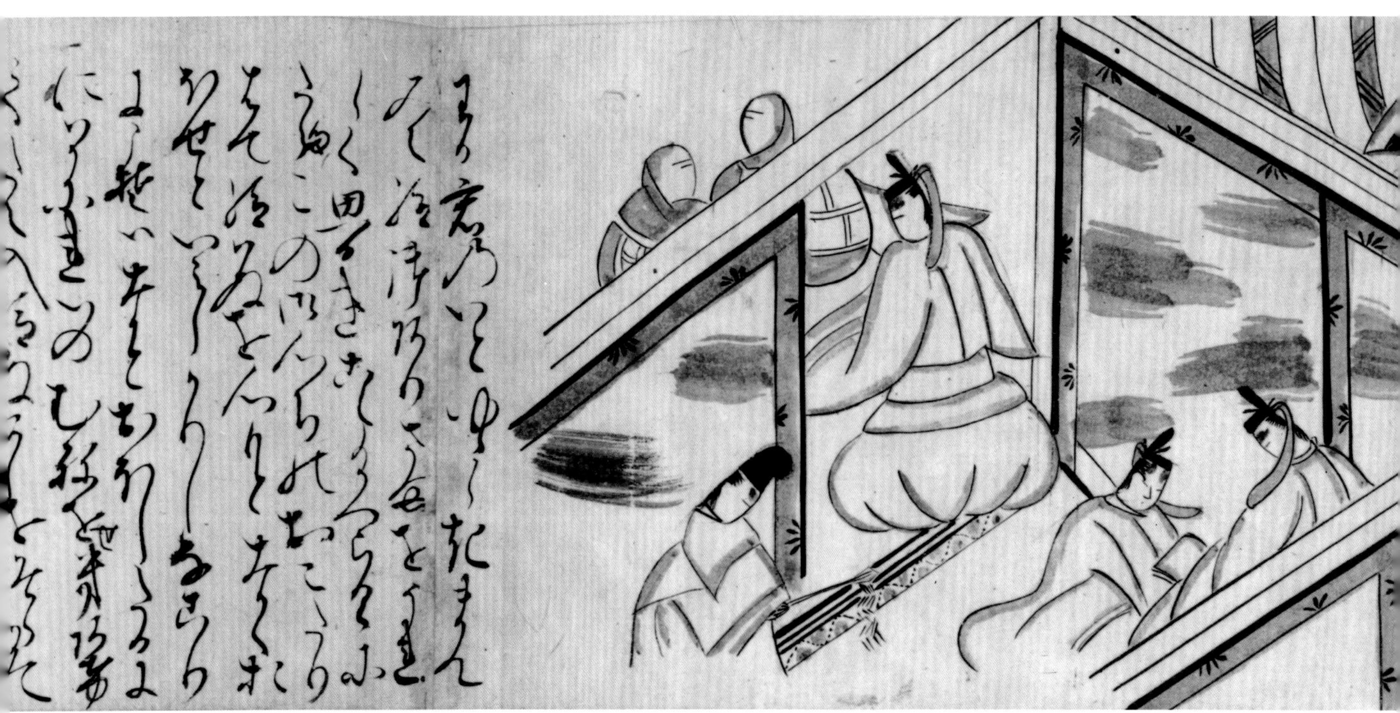

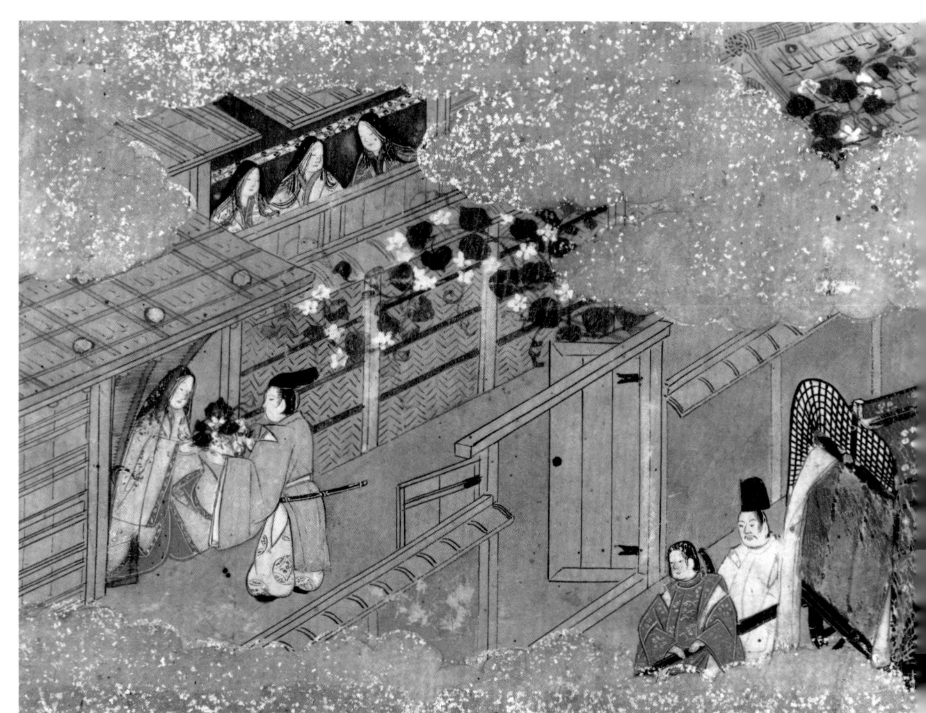

Fig. 6 / No. 22
Scenes from *The Tale of Genji*
album with 20 leaves; ink, color,
and gold on paper
Edo period, 17th century
16.4 x 21.7 cm (each leaf)

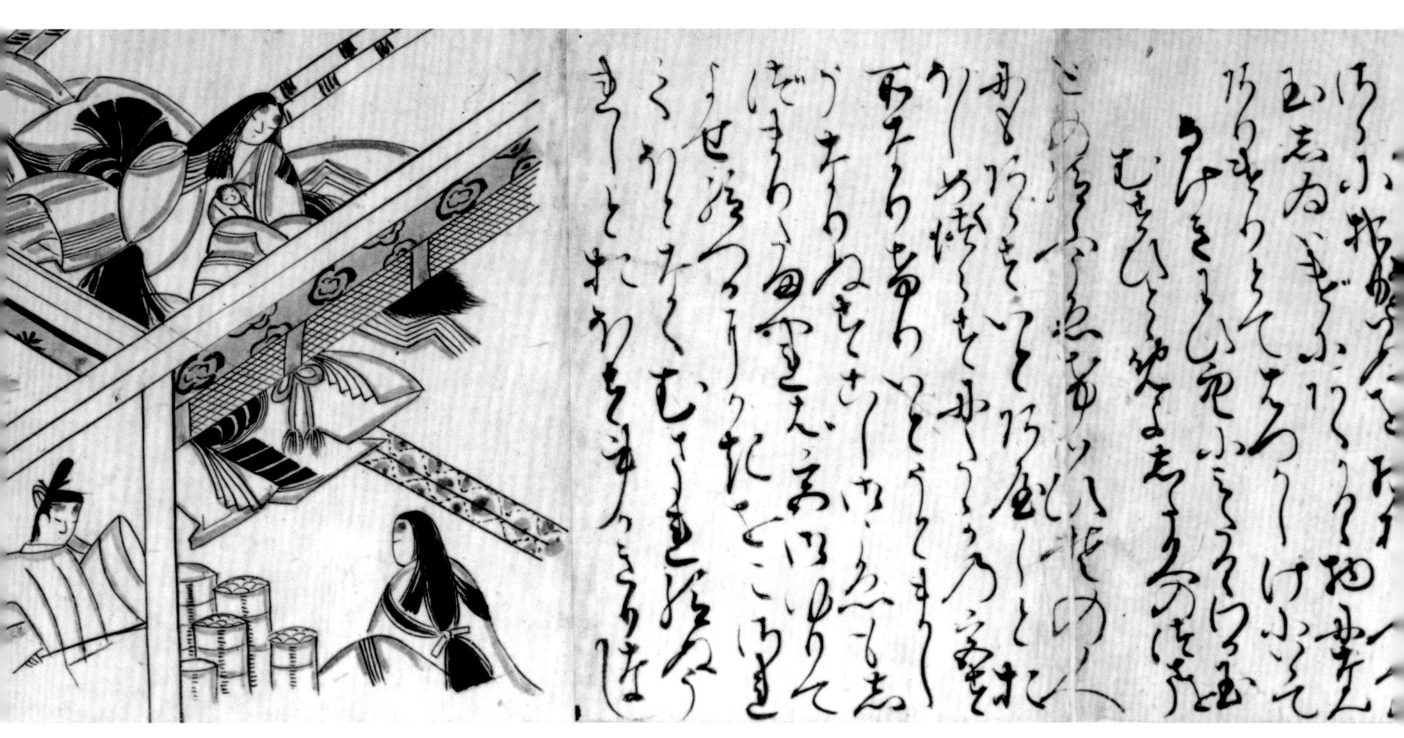

young women behind raised shutters. A little girl emerges and hands Genji's man a scented fan on which one of the flowers has been placed. On the fan, the lady of the house has inscribed a poem. This indirect encounter leads to the most tragic of Genji's romances. Genji takes the delicate and beautiful lady, symbolized by the *yūgao* flowers, to a nearby villa. There she dies in his arms, possessed by the jealous spirit of the Rokujō lady, another of his lovers.

The illustration of Chapter Twenty-five depicts Tamakazura, the daughter of the "evening faces" lady. Years after the lady's mysterious death, Genji finds Tamakazura and brings her to his house as his ward. Here, the young girl receives the attentions of Prince Hotaru, a suitor. Genji, who has put a number of fireflies into a bag, releases them in her direction while she tries to hide her face from their light.

The last of the *Genji* objects in this exhibition is a small sixteenth-century handscroll (Fig. 7/No. 19) of *hakubyō* (literally, "white drawing") paintings. *Hakubyō* first became popular during the thirteenth century; the early, classic technique does not utilize ink wash or brush lines to define planes and three-dimensionality. Instead, shapes are entirely delineated by the delicate austerity of black ink outlines executed with little or no modulation. *Hakubyō* narrative illustrations of the sixteenth and seventeenth centuries cannot match the ink line drawings of the Kamakura period (1185–1333), but the genre did survive the passage of time to become a favored mode of painting among amateur artists. Some late works tend to be technically naive, decorative small-scale paintings, executed with exuberance. The outlines vary from relatively soft and broad to thin, sharp brushstrokes that lack the fine tension characteristic of earlier *hakubyō*.

The example shown here depicts an episode from Chapter Nine, "Heartvine." In the typical "blown-off-roof" fashion of early, courtly-style illustration, this scene allows one to look in upon Genji's principal wife, Aoi, who has just given birth to Genji's son Yūgiri. Unfortunately, she dies, and it becomes apparent to Genji that his lover, the jealous Rokujō lady, has once again brought about the death of a rival. The Rokujō lady cannot control her jealous spirit or keep it from taking possession of those toward whom she feels enmity.

A less formal mode of painting (also included within the broad category of *yamato-e*) was used to illustrate native non-aristocratic tales or depict commoners and members of the rising provincial warrior class. Folk tales, religious legends, and historical accounts of important battles and dramatic episodes in the twelfth- and thirteenth-century battles for control of the government were recorded in this style. One feature which distinguishes it from the formal, decorative idiom employed for the *Genji* paintings is its wonderful use of lively, fluid ink line. In late Heian- and Kamakura-period narrative handscrolls executed in this manner, faces and other physical features are often intensely individualized to the point of caricature. These paintings stress realism and detail, movement and continuous action. Their tradition was perpetuated, in a modified state, into the Edo period. In this exhibition, the nineteenth-century handscroll entitled *Night Parade of One Hundred Demons* (Plate 4/No. 24) reflects some of the vitality and charm of earlier narrative-handscroll illustration.

This amusing handscroll, whose theme was painted numerous times between the fourteenth and nineteenth centuries, depicts one of the many versions of an ancient folk belief. According to this legend, ogres, demons, and goblins parade by night through the streets and old mansions until the light of dawn causes them to return to their nether world. Early Japanese literature records several "true encounters" of men with such demons, and at one time court regulations forbade aristocrats from venturing outside at night for fear of meeting these frightening creatures. The old folk belief that worn-out household utensils and tools can be transformed into evil demons is also illustrated in this painting.

This *Demons* scroll entered the Burke Collection quite recently. At that time, I planned a costume party for which guests were asked to appear as Japanese demons or mythical creatures. My Curator even based her costume on a demon in the scroll, and all of the guests joined in the "night parade."

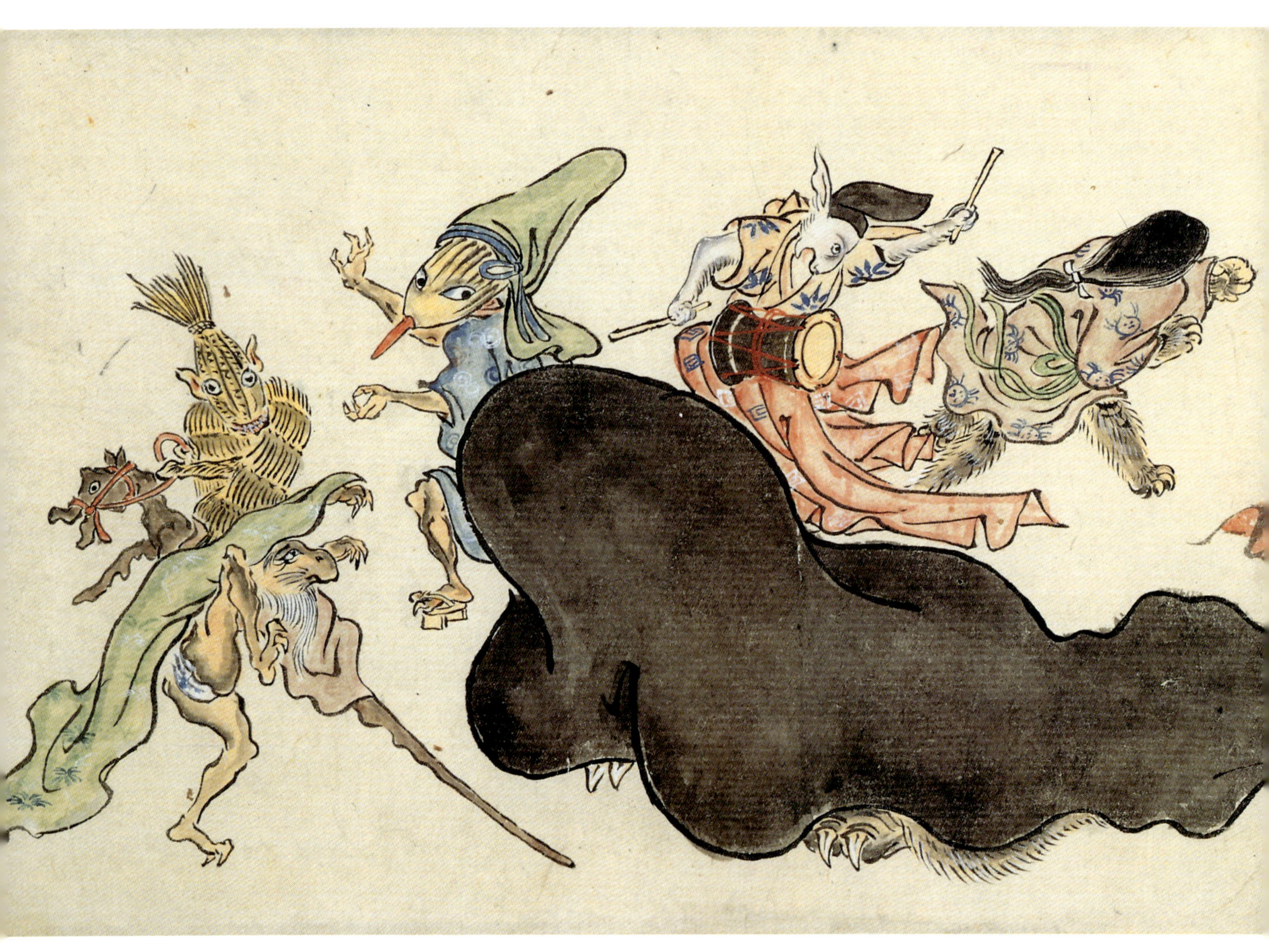

Plate 4 (detail) / No. 24
Night Parade of
One Hundred Demons
handscroll; ink and color on paper
Edo period, 19th century
23.2 x 488.4 cm

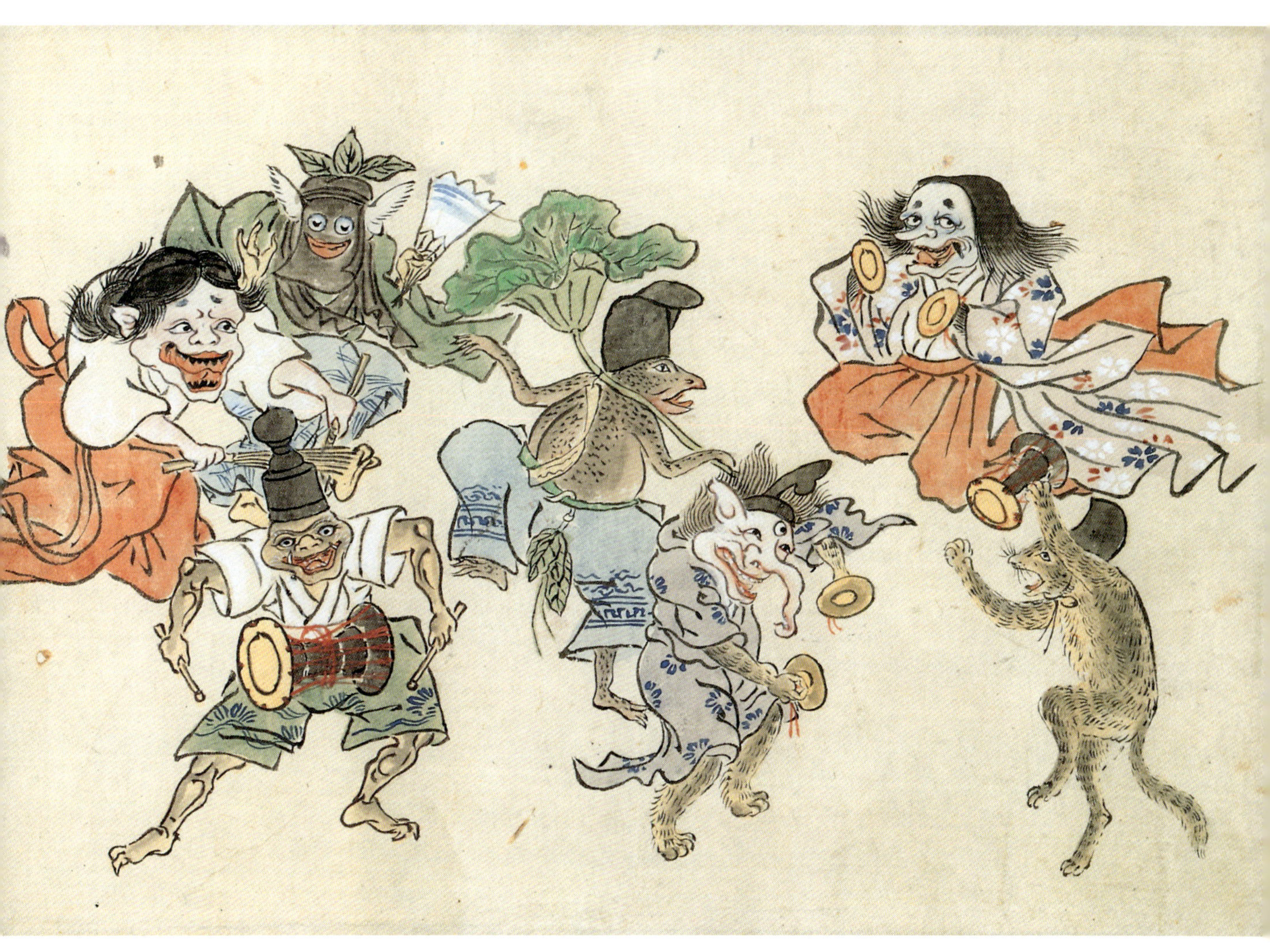

The Aesthetics of Ink: Muromachi through Edo

The second great wave of Chinese culture came to Japan in the thirteenth century. Like the first, it brought Buddhist influence, but this type of Buddhism—Zen—was quite different from the esoteric sects imported in earlier times. Zen focused on contemplative meditation and the study of *kōan* (paradoxical statements or puzzles that cannot be solved by common logic) as the means of eliminating all illusions which obscure the path to enlightenment.

Zen's simplicity and directness, and its emphasis on self-discipline, made it particularly attractive to literate members of the *samurai* (warrior) class. Moreover, since Zen prelates—many of whom had visited China—were familiar with such Chinese institutions as Confucianism, their advice was sought by military rulers in conducting affairs of state. Zen thus became the most powerful religious force in Japan during the Muromachi period, which encompassed two turbulent centuries, from the late fourteenth to the late sixteenth.

At this time, the warrior government (the shogunate) was located in the Muromachi district of Kyoto, to the northwest of the old Imperial Palace. The Ashikaga family, which dominated the shogunal office, produced a number of leaders who were outstanding for their superb artistic tastes, if not for their political acumen. Under the reign of the third Ashikaga shogun, Yoshimitsu (1358–1408), Zen and the arts flourished. Yoshimasa (1435–1490), who followed him, was another patron of the arts. It was Yoshimasa's instructor in the tea ceremony, Murata Jukō (1422–1502), who promoted the aesthetics of *wabi* and *sabi*, the "forlorn" and "rustic" beauty of imperfection which draws, as Miyeko Murase has written,

> many elements of the arts connected with the cult of tea into a harmonious whole. At its highest level, the tea ceremony involves the appreciation of garden design, architecture, interior design, calligraphy, painting, flower arrangement, and all the minor arts ... It is a truly unique experience of many levels of beauty and taste within the microcosm of a tea room, and the participant's state of mind must be attuned ... to be drawn into communion with all the arts that surround him ... The aesthetic tradition thus established left a deep impression on the Japanese, and it still affects their lives today.
>
> Miyeko Murase, *Japanese Art: Selections from the Mary and Jackson Burke Collection*, 1975, pp. 86–87

The vogue in painting inspired by Zen was ink monochrome, or *suibokuga*, literally "picture" *(ga)* of "water" *(sui)* and "ink" *(boku)*. In Japan early practitioners of *suibokuga* were Zen monks, some of whom traveled to China to learn the art. Technical characteristics of ink painting made it an ideal medium for the spontaneous and spiritual expression of Zen. The inked brush must be applied without hesitation, and with total concentration, to the paper or silk. No correction is possible. This style of painting requires vigorous training and complete mastery of the brush. The fact that, in general, only ink tones are used does away with the sensual distractions of color. Early ink paintings by Japanese artists included works based on imported Chinese paintings or on themes introduced from China. Among the subjects were Zen masters and patriarchs, more traditional Buddhist figures like Śākyamuni (the historical Buddha), the bodhisattva Kannon, and eccentrics from Zen lore. Non-religious scenes of landscape and bird-and-flower compositions also became part of the Zen artist's repertoire.

As Zen ink painting was assimilated into Japanese culture it became increasingly secular. Landscape themes began to dominate the genre, and in the late fifteenth century artists like the great master Sesshū (1420–1506) broke away from earlier standards, turning to subject matter that emphasized aesthetic appeal over spiritual content. Thus *suibokuga* was gradually adapted to suit native taste, and it emerged by the end of the fifteenth century as part of the mainstream of Japanese art. Broadened by its absorption of elements from native styles of painting, *suibokuga* in turn enriched the native tradition, first as the medium of choice of the Chinese-influenced Kano artists and later as an inspiration for other schools of painting. Some works classified as *suibokuga* do have light washes of color, while many paintings from later periods—such as decorative screens and Nanga (literati) school works—although executed in ink do not adhere to the spiritual foundation of Zen.

One mode of abbreviated brushwork, in which a few bold strokes suggest external form and inner character, was developed in the thirteenth century and used mainly by Zen monks. Although Zen *suibokuga* lost some of its impact during the first hundred years of the Edo period, it was revived in the eighteenth century in the form of *Zenga*, a mode of painting closely associated with calligraphy. *Zenga* artists were primarily monks, trained in calligraphy from childhood, who produced spontaneous, powerful works unencumbered by the standards of painting schools or traditions. The most influential of these artists was Hakuin Ekaku (1685–1769), who became a Zen monk at the age of fifteen. As a Zen scholar, writer, and teacher Hakuin gave new impetus to the spirit of Japanese Zen, but he did not begin to paint until he was over sixty years of age. The painting by Hakuin illustrated here (Fig. 8/No. 7) bears his seals and a very brief title inscription that reads "The First Dream." Such inscriptions, sometimes written by the artist and sometimes by another calligrapher, were always designed to clarify the meaning of the image and enhance the composition. Hakuin's painting beautifully illustrates the spontaneity and spareness of Zen painting, employing an economy of means to present its theme. Several versions of this picture exist, each containing the same motifs: Mount Fuji, a hawk feather or two and eggplants. Two are by Hakuin himself, and one is the work of Reigen Etō (1721–1785), Hakuin's disciple.

Zen painting relies on simplified symbols to convey its message, and the auspicious motifs in this work apparently refer to a good-luck expression from Suruga (present-day Shizuoka Prefecture), where Mount Fuji is located and where Hakuin was born. Indeed, the version by Reigen Etō bears an inscription, clearly derived from the popular Shizuoka saying, which refers to three specialties of the region.

Ichi, Fuji	Number one, Fuji
Ni, taka	Number two, a hawk
San, nasubi	Number three, eggplants
	Koji kotowaza jiten, 1983, p. 48

The "First Dream" inscription on the Burke Collection's Hakuin painting gives the clue that the work depicts a New Year's dream, believed to be of great importance as an auspicious harbinger of what was in store for the ensuing twelve months.

Another interpretation, given to Reigen Etō's painting by John Stevens, reads as follows: "The best dream is of Mt. Fuji. Fuji also symbolizes great ambition that reaches towards the clouds. Just as a hawk seizes the opportunity to capture its prey, we should act boldly in order to attain good fortune. A field of eggplants represents realization of all one's dreams. In short, Zen—symbolized by the majestic form of Mt. Fuji—is a field of good fortune for those who grasp its essence" (Stevens, *Zenga: Brushstrokes of Enlightenment*, 1990, p. 158).

Hakuin's second extant version of this theme belongs to the Tenkyū-in of Myōshinji temple in Kyoto. It is almost identical to the painting in the Burke Collection, except that its inscription is a combination of the inscriptions on the Burke painting and the Reigen Etō work.

Another interpretation of this image is given by Yasuichi Awakawa in his book *Zen Painting*. He believes that Mount Fuji symbolizes the famous revenge of the Soga brothers on the murderer of their father, an act carried out at the mountain itself. The crossed hawk feathers are also a revenge symbol; they form the crest of Lord Asano (1665–1701), whose death was avenged by his forty-seven loyal retainers. Awakawa believes that the eggplants represent the revenge of the *samurai* Araki Mataemon (1599–1638), as Mataemon

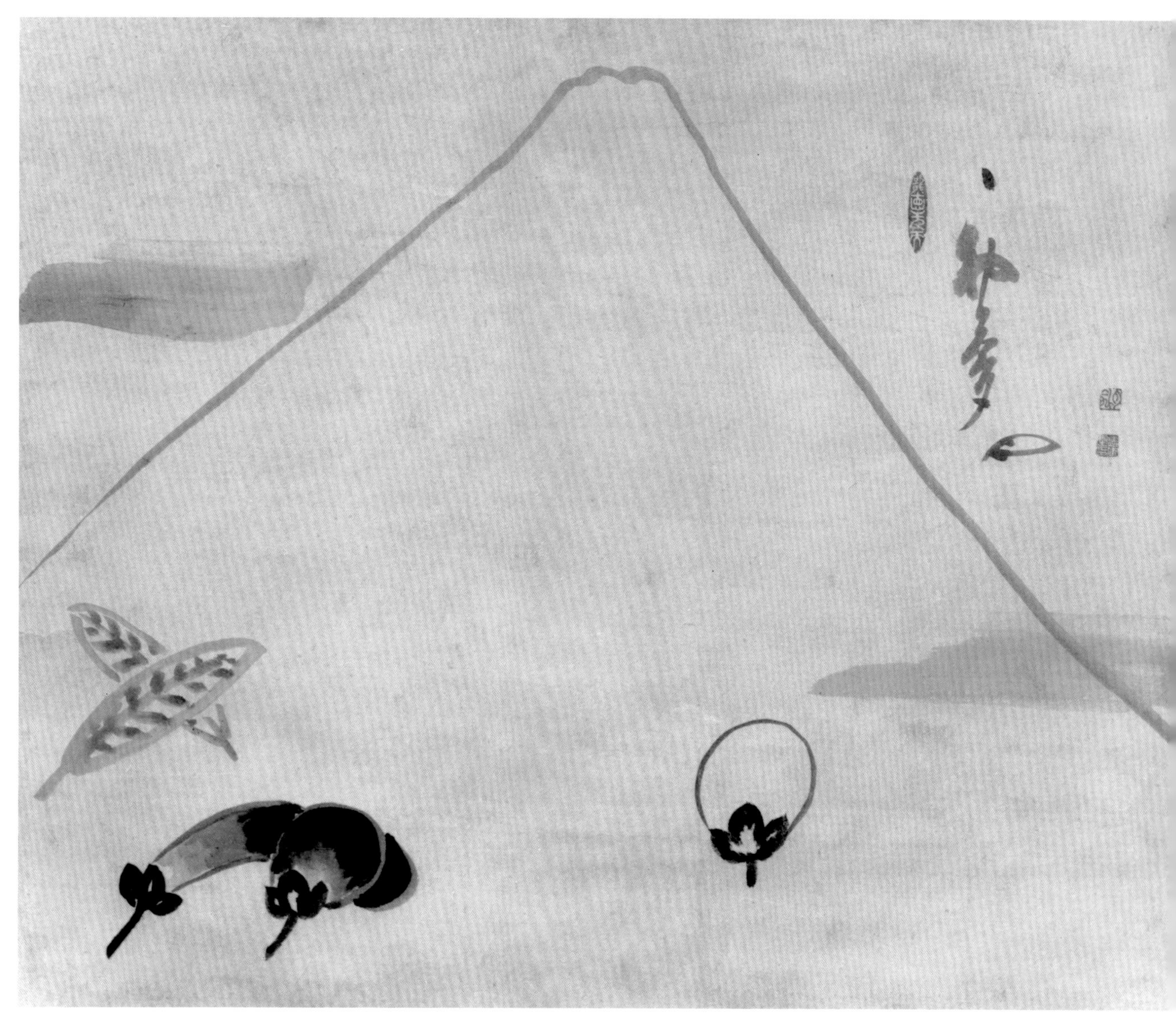

Fig. 8 / No. 7
Dream of the New Year
by Hakuin (1685–1768)
Cipher: Hakuin
Seals: Ryūtoku Senten, Hakuin, Ekaku-no-in
hanging scroll; ink on paper
Edo period, 18th century
52.0 x 64.6 cm

avenged the death of a friend during the tenth month, when eggplants are at their best. Awakawa interprets the message of this painting and its inscription as follows: "So long as one is free from wrongful thoughts and illusions, one's very dreams... will be trouble free" (Awakawa, *Zen Painting*, 1970, p. 128).

It appears to me that imagination plays a larger role than fact in the interpretations assigned to this fascinating image. Some interpretations of these paintings and their cryptic inscriptions remind me of intensely personal responses to the ink-blot Rorschach test.

In order to appreciate fully another mode of ink painting, exemplified here by the work of Kano Tan'yū, it is necessary to consider the development of the Kano school, which sprang from Chinese-influenced *suibokuga* in the late Muromachi and Momoyama (1573–1615) periods. This school was founded by Kano Masanobu (1434–1530) and continued by his son Motonobu (1476–1559). Masanobu was appointed painter-in-attendance to the Muromachi shogunate, becoming the first strictly secular and professional artist to benefit from the stylistic tradition and patronage previously claimed by Zen monk-painters. The Kano school grew into a vast network of artists, linked by family ties and training. For nearly 250 years it held a virtual monopoly of public and private commissions from the shogunate, affluent monasteries, provincial warlords, and merchants newly risen to wealth and social prominence.

Motonobu ensured the school's continuing prosperity by establishing an orthodox "Kano style" and instituting a studio system to guarantee the professionalism of Kano-trained artists. This style, based on Chinese ink painting, was also characterized by a decorative quality (at times enhanced by brilliant colors and gold) derived, in part, from the native tradition of *yamato-e*.

During the Momoyama period, often called the "Age of Grandeur," this mode of painting flourished. The political order was transformed, and the activities of European traders and missionaries in Japan, as well as Japanese ventures overseas, greatly expanded the country's horizons. To understand this era it is necessary to appreciate the joint use of power and the arts. The strong, lavishly decorated Momoyama castles were symbolic of the age. They were meant more for display, and the glorification of their owners, than for military defense against newly introduced firearms. Kano Eitoku (1543–1590) and other members of the Kano family decorated the fortress interiors with paintings of heroic motifs, such as large pines and cypress trees, peonies, hawks, dragons, lions, and tigers. Unfortunately, not many castles survived the battles of this tumultuous era, and only a few sections of buildings and screens removed from their original sites hint at their splendor.

Eitoku created a heroic style that was one of the chief glories of the Kano tradition. During the Edo period, however, Kano Tan'yū (1602–1794) revived the fifteenth-century *suibokuga* roots of the school. Here he is represented by a small album (Fig. 9/No. 21) depicting the *Eight Views of the Hsiao and Hsiang Rivers*, a Chinese theme frequently painted by Kano artists. It is a fine example of the "splash-ink" technique of ink painting so dear to the hearts of Zen artists in the earlier Muromachi period. The subject of painting in China from at least the eleventh century on, the *Eight Views*, with their poetic, evocative titles, were meant to be expressive of the interactive forces of nature, the seasons, and man within the lush, watery regions of what is now Hunan Province. More specifically, they focus on the site, rich in history and literary allusion, where the Hsiao and Hsiang rivers converge to flow northward into Lake Tung-t'ing. In the leaf shown here, the poetic inscription, *Evening Bell at the Temple in Smoky Mist*, places an otherwise nonspecific scene within a particular context as one of the famous views. The "splash-ink" method successfully portrays a mountainous landscape shrouded in mist. The only clearly defined object, the temple, establishes the setting. This and the seven other paintings in the album—*Wild Geese Descending to a Sand Bar, Mountain Village in a Clearing Haze, Autumn Moon over Lake Tung-t'ing, Evening Snow on the Lake and Hills, Night Rain at Hsiao-Hsiang, Evening Glow on a Fishing Village*, and *Homeward-bound Fishing Boats*—are accompanied by poems. The verse on the page facing the "Evening Bell" scene has been translated as follows:

Kurekakaru	At sunset
Kiri yori tsutau	The temple bell sounds
Kane no ne ni	Through the fog;
Ochikatabito mo	People in distant places, too,
Michi isogu nari.	Hurry on their way.
	Trans. Fumiko E. Cranston

It was common for images of the *Eight Views* to be accompanied by poems. (Ms. Cranston has pointed out that some versions of the "Evening Bell" poem contain the characters for "distant temple" rather than "temple in smoky mist.")

Another Kano work in this exhibition, *The Bodhisattva Monju* (Plate 5/No. 4), once may have formed part of a triptych with images of the historical Buddha and the bodhisattva Fugen. Its style is derived from early Buddhist figure painting, as Buddhist imagery formed part of the repertoire of the Kano school. The artist, Kiyohara Yukinobu (1643–1682), was a grandniece of Tan'yū. Both her father and her husband were Tan'yū's pupils, and she herself may have studied with him. His stylistic influence can be seen in her use of fluid brushstrokes and light color. The deity, who symbolizes the wisdom and spirituality of the Buddha, is shown seated on a lion, holding a scroll containing the "Greater Sutra [sacred text] of the Perfection of Wisdom." Gratia Williams Nakahashi has said of this

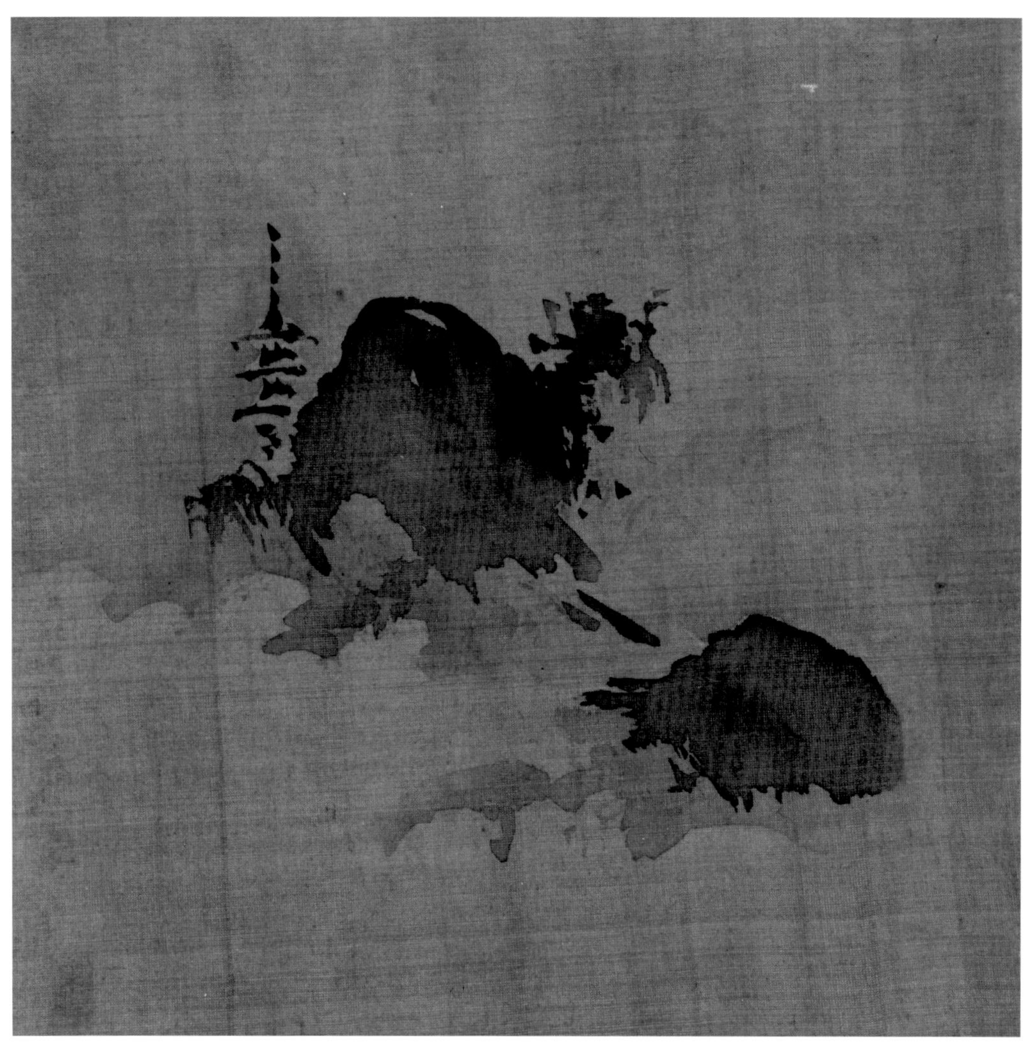

Fig. 9 / No. 21
Eight Views of the Hsiao and Hsiang Rivers
by Kano Tan'yū (1602–1674)
Seal: Tan'yū
album with 8 leaves; ink on silk
Edo period, 17th century
Ptg. 17.8 x 17.4 cm (each leaf)
Call. 19.5 x 18.5 cm (each leaf)

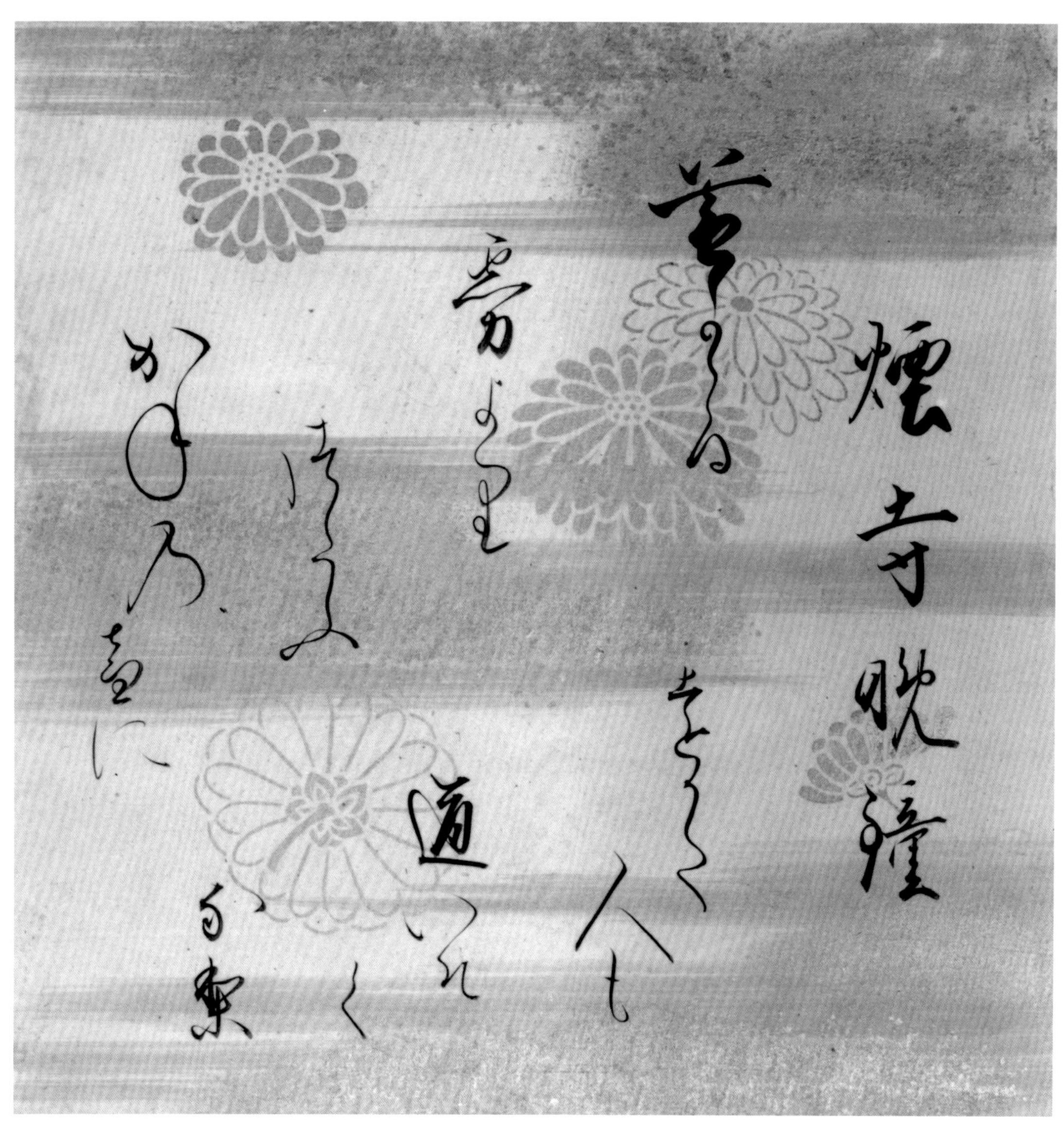
煙寺晩鐘

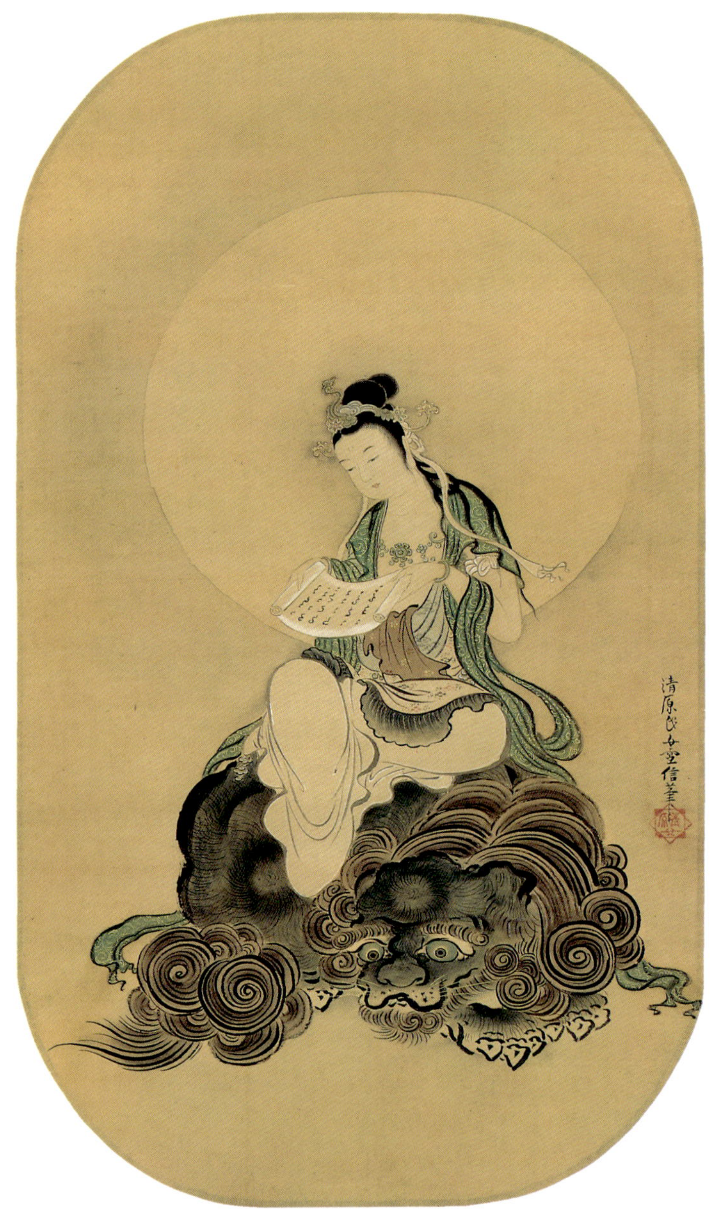

Plate 5 / No. 4
The Bodhisattva Monju
by Kiyohara Yukinobu (1643–1682)
Signature: Kiyohara-shi no musume
Yukinobu hitsu
Seal: Kiyohara-jo
hanging scroll; color, ink, and
gold on silk
Edo period, 17th century
62.4 x 36.0 cm

painting: "The especially feminine appearance of Monju—due perhaps to the gender of the painter—is enhanced by the ornaments which embellish the coiffure and the beautifully detailed patterns on the robes delineated with delicate applications of color and gold. The imaginary lion, a frequent companion to Monju, is portrayed as a docile rather than a ferocious creature" (trans. Gratia Williams Nakahashi, from Gunhild Avitabile, ed., *Die Kunst des alten Japan*, 1990, p. 76).

These paintings by Kano Tan'yū and Kiyohara Yukinobu do not give one a sense of the strength and glory of the monumental landscapes, figure paintings, and bird-and-flower compositions for which the Kano school was renowned. One must bear in mind, however, that as professional painters Kano artists produced works of great variety, in formats ranging from fans, handscrolls, and albums to small votive plaques. The less grandiose works are also indicative of the stylistic and thematic range of the Kano school. By adapting their style to suit native themes, Kano artists were able to assume a leading role as painters for the imperial court as well as the shogunate.

Diversity in Style and Subject: Momoyama through Edo

In spite of the dominance of the Kano school, other painters of the Momoyama period flourished and vied with the Kano for commissions. Among the artistic schools which began to evolve in Momoyama times, one stands out in notable contrast to the Kano. In the beginning it was comprised of a small, loosely-knit group of painters, designers, and craftsmen, known today as founders of the Rimpa school. These artists produced paintings, calligraphy, ceramics, and lacquer designs. They came together through shared artistic aspirations; inclusion in their group was not based on birthright, although some family ties were established among them through marriage.

Hon'ami Kōetsu (1558–1635) and Tawaraya Sōtatsu (d. ca. 1643) were the actual founders of the school. Kōetsu, who came from a wealthy merchant-class Kyoto family, was a distinguished calligrapher, *chanoyu* (tea ceremony) practitioner, and accomplished potter, as well as a designer of papers, lacquer decoration, and metalwork. Like many calligraphers of his time he was influenced by the aesthetics of the late Heian period.

Unfortunately, little documentary evidence is available about Kōetsu's sometime collaborator Sōtatsu, the originator of Rimpa-style painting. It is known that he headed the Tawaraya workshop in Kyoto, which made and sold fans as well as other painted objects. Because of his prodigious talent, Sōtatsu eventually advanced to the status of a professional painter. For many of his paintings he found inspiration in native Japanese sources, specifically the *yamato-e* images of the Heian period. His own work is bold and dramatic, with a tendency toward asymmetry of composition and deliberate simplicity of silhouette. At times, he created a rich, purely decorative surface by limiting his palette to gold and silver.

The pair of screens entitled *Islands and Pines* (Plate 6/No. 25) exhibit some stylistic features of Sōtatsu's paintings. They are signed "Sōtatsu Hokkyō" and bear the "Taisei-ken" seal associated with his work. However, they are probably from the hand of one or more of the artists in Sōtatsu's atelier, rather than the master himself. The application of *tarashikomi*—a pooling together of colors and ink—is a signature technique of the Rimpa school. Extensive use of gold dust and *noge* (strips of silver leaf), the decorative wave patterns and modeling of rocks and azaleas with touches of color give a sense of the sumptuousness that characterizes many Rimpa screens. These are evidently closely related to the well-known *Matsushima* screens by Sōtatsu at the Freer Gallery in Washington, D.C.

Tawaraya Sōsetsu (fl. 1639–1650) may have been Sōtatsu's younger brother or son. Whether or not a family tie existed, their works are stylistically very close. Temple records indicate that Sōsetsu inherited Sōtatsu's shop and honorary title. The composition of chrysanthemums attributed to Sōsetsu (Fig. 10/No. 3), shown here, was probably once part of a set of paintings depicting flora of the four seasons. No ink lines are used to delineate the plant leaves, but dark ink, applied over light wash, creates a smudged, *tarashikomi* effect.

The small fan-shaped painting *Utsu no yama* (Fig. 11/No. 5), attributed to Fukae Roshū (1699–1757), is an example of eighteenth-century Rimpa, yet it adheres closely to the style of Sōtatsu. It depicts an episode from Chapter Nine of *The Tales of Ise (Ise Monogatari)*, a tenth-century literary classic that predates the more famous *Tale of Genji* by several decades. A young courtier has left the capital and is journeying to a distant province; on Mount Utsu, he follows a dark, narrow road overgrown with vines of ivy and maples. As he contemplates it with foreboding, a wandering ascetic appears. The courtier recognizes him as an old acquaintance and gives him a message for a lady in the capital.

Little is known about Roshū's life except that he studied briefly under the Rimpa master Ōgata Kōrin (1658–1716). At the age of sixteen he was banished from Edo in the wake of a scandal at the government mint which involved several officials, including his father and his patron. Although cut off from further instruction, Roshū continued to paint in the Rimpa style, choosing to work in a mode influenced more closely by Sōtatsu than by Kōrin.

The regime established by the Tokugawa shogunate of the Edo period provided Japan with over two centuries of freedom from internal strife. Despite restrictive measures employed by the shogunate, Edo society experienced significant changes in political organization, social structure, its economy and culture in general. The most dramatic change was the spread of urban development. With the appearance in the sixteenth century of unified *daimyo* (feudal lord) domains and the movement of *samurai* into urban areas, regional castle towns sprang up rapidly. As *samurai* made the transition from military duty to civil bureaucratic service, they became more cultured, better educated, and citified. Newly affluent townspeople developed a vigorous popular culture of their own, which centered around the theater district and the licensed pleasure quarters. During the Edo period, artists enjoyed a greater freedom of movement because of the recently constructed national network of highways. It is thus not surprising that so many different schools of painting were active during this era, among them Kano, Maruyama-Shijō, Nanga, and Ukiyo-e; a number of independent artists also flourished. The Rimpa school continued to produce innovative

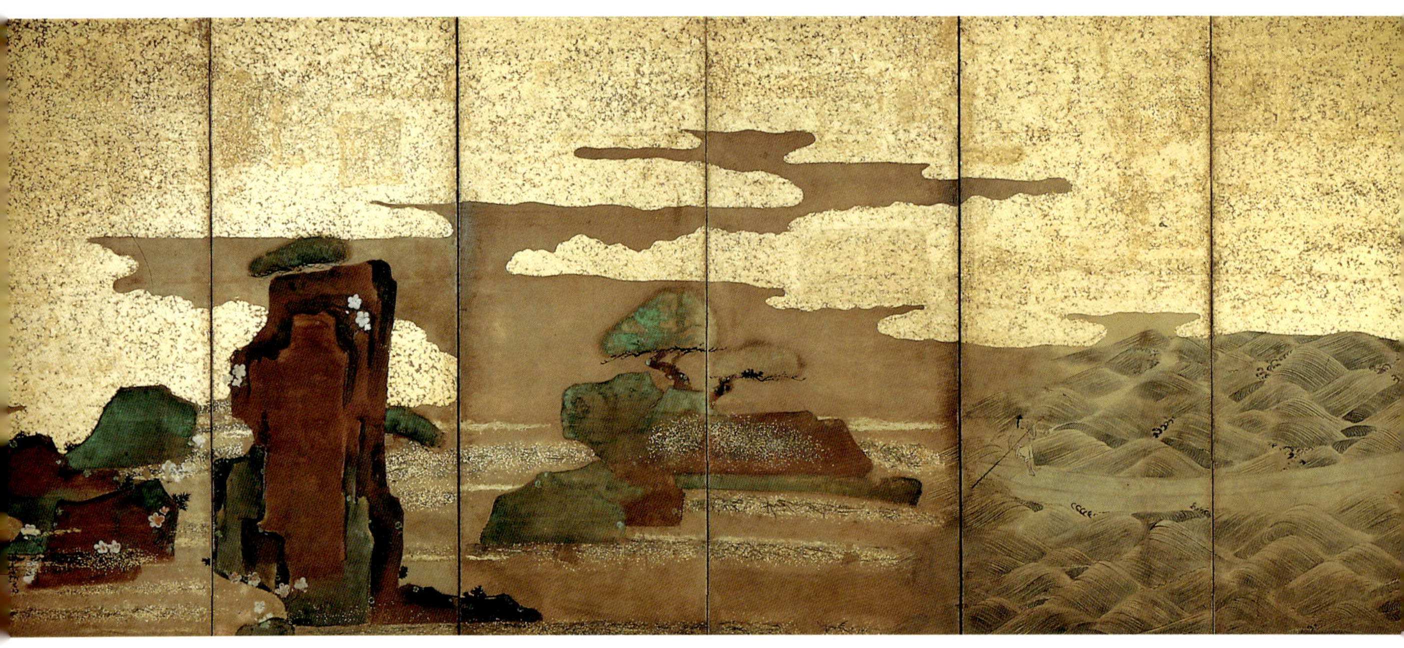

Plate 6 / No. 25
Islands and Pines
School of Sōtatsu
Signature: (each screen) Sōtatsu Hokkyō
Seal: (each screen) Taisei-ken
pair of six-fold screens; ink, color,
and gold on paper
Edo period, 17th century
154.5 x 357.8 cm (each screen)

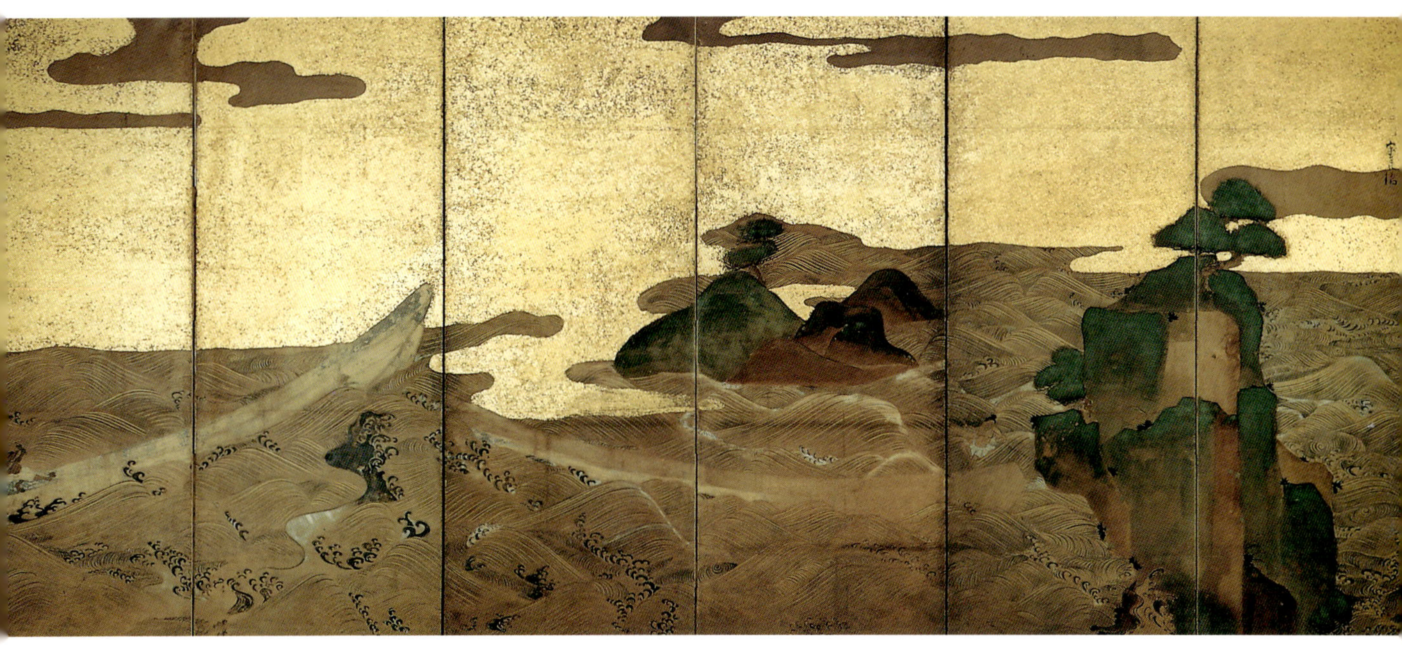

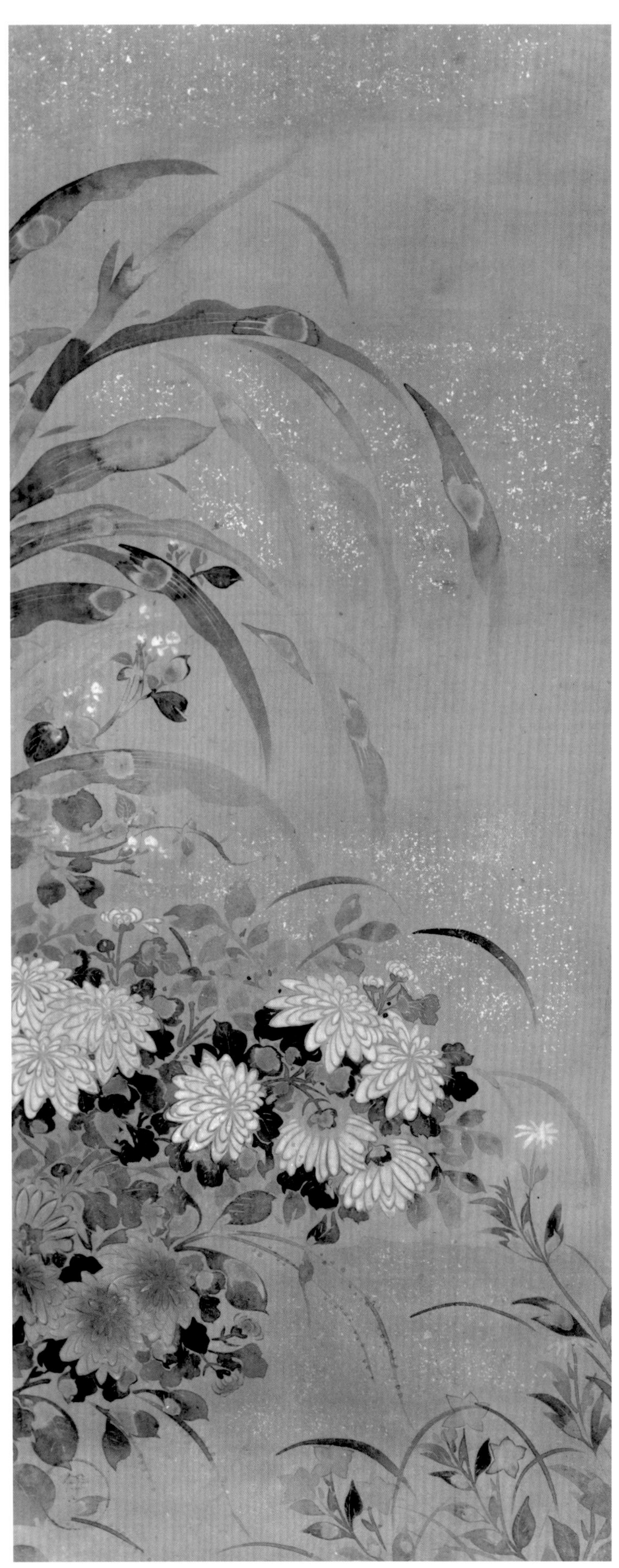

Fig. 10 / No. 3
Chrysanthemums
attributed to Tawaraya Sōsetsu
(fl. 1639–1650)
Seal: Inen
hanging scroll; ink, light color,
and gold on paper
Edo period, 17th century
123.9 x 49.8 cm

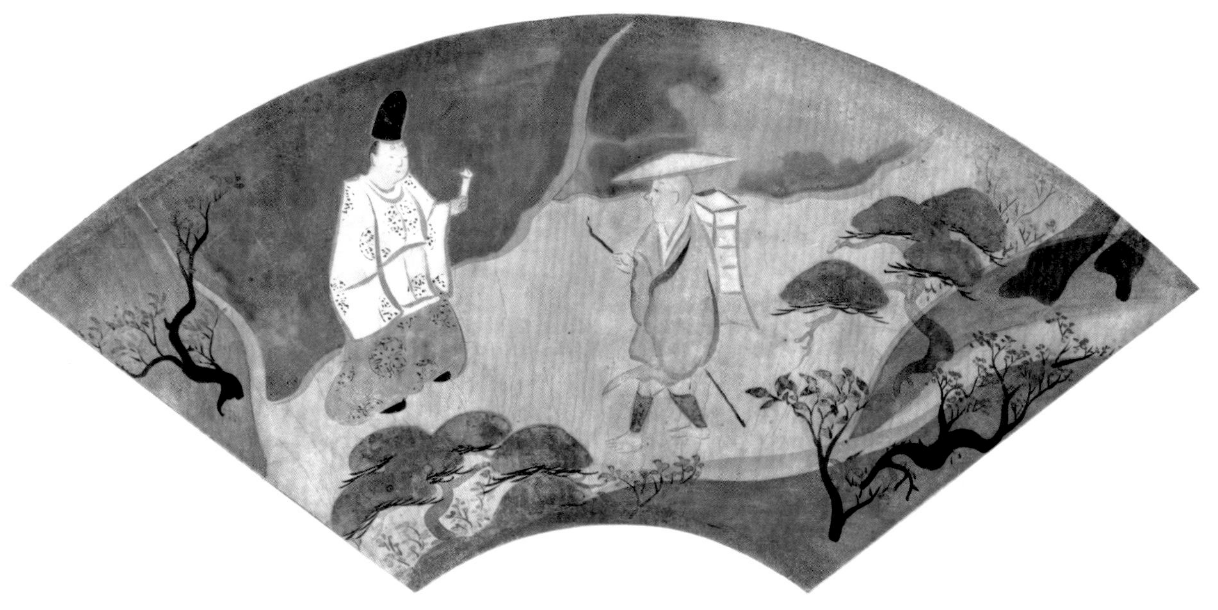

Fig. 11 / No. 5
"Utsu no yama" episode from
Chapter 9 of *The Tales of Ise*
attributed to Fukae Roshū
(1699–1757)
hanging scroll; color and
ink on paper
Edo period, 18th century
22.2 x 46.2 cm

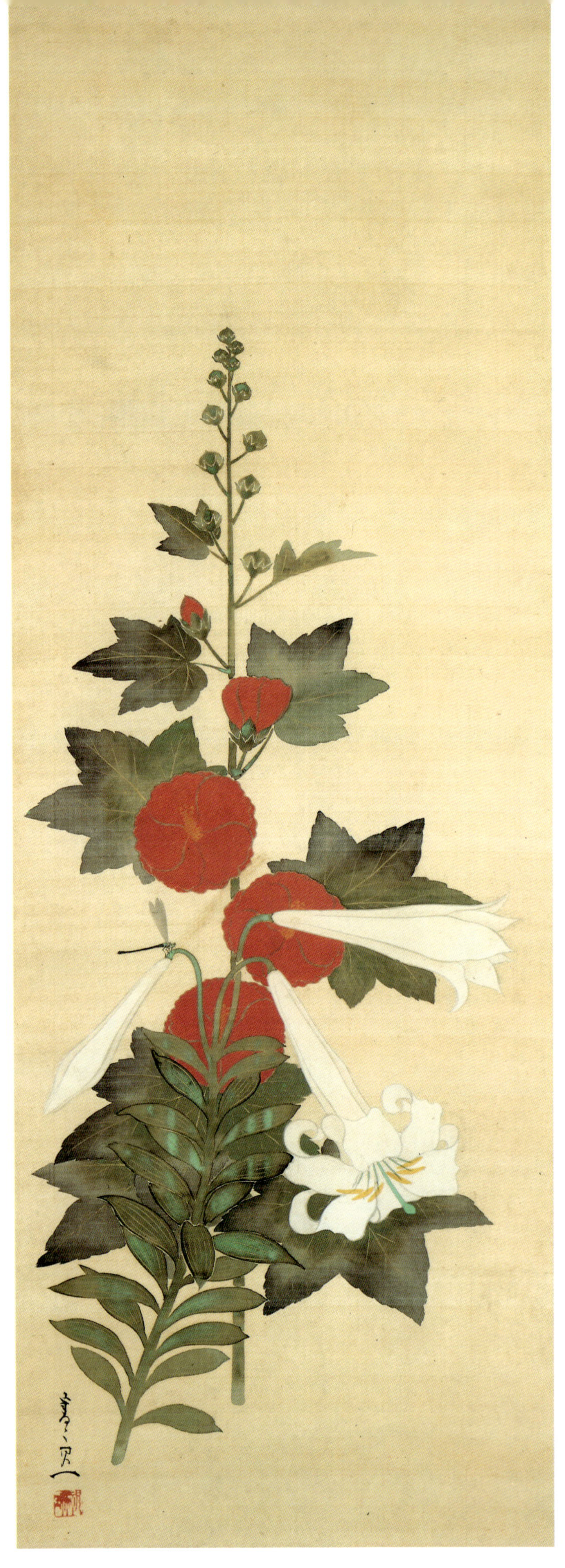

Plate 7 / No. 14
Hollyhocks and Lilies
by Suzuki Kiitsu (1796–1858)
Signature: Seisei Kiitsu
Seal: Shukurin
hanging scroll; ink, color,
and gold on silk
Edo period, 19th century
110.0 x 35.0 cm

painters, designers, and craftsmen, who—to a greater or lesser degree—followed the aesthetic tenets established by the group's founders.

Ōgata Kōrin carried on the legacy of Kōetsu and Sōtatsu, and it was during his time that the name "Rimpa," meaning school *(ha* or *pa)* of Kōrin *(rin)*, was first used. A descendant of Kōetsu's sister and member of the prosperous upper middle class, Kōrin personified the luxury-loving urban society of the later Edo period. Like Kōetsu, he worked in a variety of media, including lacquer and textile design, and he collaborated with his younger brother, the Rimpa ceramic artist/calligrapher Kenzan (1663–1843).

Sakai Hōitsu (1761–1828) carried the Rimpa school into the nineteenth century, along with Suzuki Kiitsu (1796–1858), his most gifted student, and Nakamura Hōchū (fl. 1790–1818). Kiitsu is represented here by a painting entitled *Hollyhocks and Lilies* (Plate 7/No. 14). Gold outlines the veins of leaves, and the small dragonfly clinging to a lily supplies a charming touch. Hōchū, who lived most of his life in Osaka, was heavily influenced by Kōrin's style. His small *Narcissus* painting (No. 12) in ink and color on paper, displays the technique, which he perfected, of absorbing wet color or ink from the painting surface back into the brush.

Ukiyo-e, literally "pictures of the floating world," emerged as a school of painting in the early Edo period. Highly colorful Ukiyo-e paintings (and later, inexpensive prints) were extremely popular with the urban middle class and represent, in a sense, a final flowering of the ancient native tradition of genre painting. Ukiyo-e grew out of pictures of famous sites and activities associated with the different seasons of the year. Initially, it focused on actors of the Kabuki theater or women of the pleasure quarters. In the case of the latter, intimate, close-up views became popular, with much attention paid to the intricately patterned kimonos and elaborate hairstyles. The ladies were depicted engaged in such gentle pastimes as writing, reading, playing games, or promenading in their gorgeous costumes. Occasionally, allusions to classical literature or folk tales can be discerned in these worldly images. For instance, in the two-paneled screen by Tsukioka Settei (1710–1786), one panel of which is shown here (Plate 8/No. 27), we find what may be a reference to the Nō play *Matsukaze,* by Kan'ami (1333–1384). This drama, a popular subject for Edo-period painters, was based on a celebrated legend about Ariwara no Yukihira, a ninth-century courtier-poet. Temporarily banished to Suma, near the modern-day city of Kobe, the poet encounters two sisters, the brine-gathering maidens Matsukaze (Wind in the Pines) and Murasame (Autumn Showers). Both girls fall in love with him and become his mistresses. When he is pardoned and returns to court, he leaves his cap and robe with the sisters as a pledge to send for them. Back in the capital, the poet dies and the sisters await

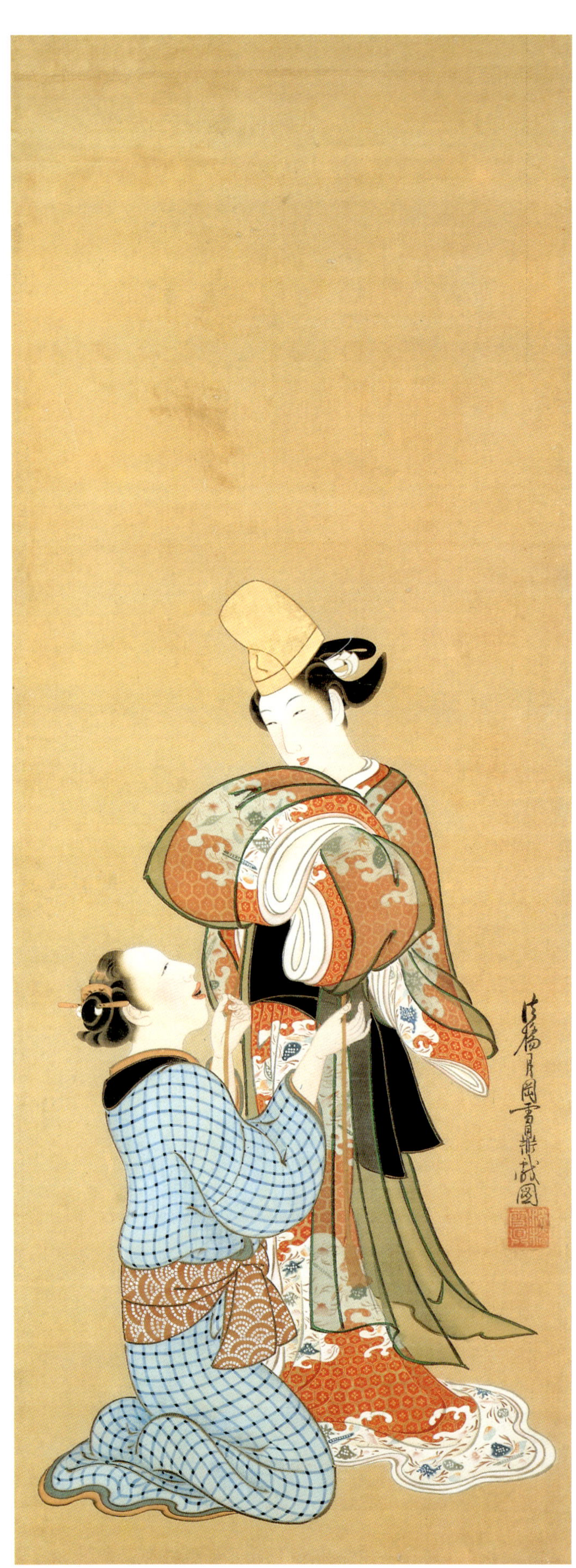

Plate 8 (detail) / No. 27
Two Beauties
by Tsukioka Settei (1710–1786)
Signature: (each panel) Hokkyō Tsukioka
Settei tawamure ni egaku
Seal: (each panel) Hokkyō Settei
two-fold screen; ink and color on silk
Edo period, 18th century
114.3 x 41.9 cm (each panel)

his return in vain. Grief-stricken, they drown themselves in the sea.

In the Nō play, this tragic tale is presented through the eyes of a traveling monk. At Suma, he is told by a villager that a large pine tree marks the place where the two sisters lived with their lover. The monk has a vision in which the sisters appear, their souls still bound to earth by their passion. Matsukaze dons the robe and cap of the courtier and embraces the pine tree as though it were Yukihira. With the coming of dawn, the sisters disappear.

On the screen, a plainly dressed woman kneels before a standing lady clad in a robe decorated with waves—a reference to the ocean and the sisters, who distill salt from sea water for a living. I assume that this character, representing Matsukaze, is about to perform the tragic dance in which she mistakes a pine tree for her lover. This scene might even be set in a brothel, with a courtesan or entertainer assuming the title role.

One of the most sumptuous pieces in this exhibition is the richly colored handscroll (Plate 9/No. 23) attributed to Ō'oka Michinobu (fl. 1720–1740). It displays a series of scenes from the largest and most important of the licensed pleasure quarters in Edo—the Yoshiwara (literally, "reed field"). Destroyed by a fire in 1657, the Yoshiwara was subsequently moved to a spacious tract in the eastern part of the city. It was not simply a collection of brothels but a highly stratified and complex world that provided a sophisticated level of entertainment. It allowed men from all classes of society the opportunity to escape social restrictions and regulations. The scroll, which is divided into five parts, begins with the arrival of flat-bottomed boats, crossing the Ōkawa (the lower reaches of the Sumida River) to deposit passengers at the only gate to the walled district (enclosed to keep customers from sneaking away without paying and to prevent courtesans from escaping). The second section shows various tea shops and lower-class prostitutes, displayed behind vertical wooden bars. *Samurai*, wearing large straw hats to hide their identity, stroll by with other patrons. The third section deals with activities in a higher-class establishment, where "ladies" are partially hidden behind woven reed curtains. A high-class courtesan passes, surrounded by her retinue of small girls, an older woman, and male servants. In the fourth section, the outer rooms of a brothel are seen. The proprietress converses with clients, women primp, and a giant fish is prepared in the kitchen. The fifth section, illustrated here, gives an account of what might happen in the "inner rooms" of such an establishment. At the extreme right, two courtesans relax, one sleeping, the other languidly strumming a *shamisen*. In the next room, a most unpleasant incident occurs. A prestigious client has become displeased with the woman of his choice. Grim-faced, he turns toward the open door, overgarment in hand to make his exit. A small girl attendant and the proprietor kneeling in front of him try to dissuade him from leaving. The courtesan—the object of his wrath—

crouches disconsolately by the table where he has been eating and buries her face in a paper handkerchief.

The style of the handscroll is pure Ukiyo-e. An emphasis is placed upon the marvelously patterned kimonos rather than the faces. The artist has applied touches of silver and gold in many areas to add to the atmosphere of sensuous luxury. The composition was evidently derived from a handscroll executed by the genre painter Hanabusa Itchō (1652–1724) in 1703, although the style of the earlier artist is much more realistic and fluid (see plates 45 and 46 in Kobayashi Tadashi, and Sakakibara Satoru, *Morikage and Itchō*, 1978).

Like Ukiyo-e, Nanga proved to be one of the most dynamic schools of the Edo period, although it took a completely different approach to pictorial representation. Ukiyo-e appealed primarily to the pleasure-seeking middle class, while Nanga, the school of the literati, sprang from a renewed interest in Chinese culture and spoke to the more scholarly elements of Japanese society. It was perhaps the last product of Japan's long-standing preoccupation with China.

The term "Nanga" (literally, "southern painting") is used interchangeably with *bunjinga* (literati painting) and derives from a concept established by the Chinese painter-critic Tung Ch'i-ch'ang (1555–1636). Tung divided the artists of China into two groups, Northern and Southern, an arrangement which had nothing to do with geographical distinctions. Into the "Southern" category, he placed the educated gentleman-painters (himself included), who did not necessarily paint to earn a living and therefore could be more self-expressive than artists who worked under patronage. Professional and academic painters, whose styles Tung regarded as laborious, superficial, or devoid of the inner truth of the subject matter, were categorized as "Northern" artists.

In spite of the Edo government's ban on contact with foreigners, some Chinese paintings of uneven quality reached Japan through the port of Nagasaki, along with a small number of Chinese woodblock-printed books. The latter, which included treatises on painting, introduced the Japanese to the concept of Nanga. Japanese artists who tried to follow these Chinese ideals had only a limited understanding of them and of the long and complex tradition of Chinese scholar-painters. They attempted to educate themselves in the manner of their Chinese predecessors; most, however, were not true literati. Some earned their living by painting, and many were in the service of feudal lords. Few had the financial means to enable them to follow the life of a gentleman-scholar.

Not surprisingly, Nanga artists turned to Chinese themes and subject matter, with an emphasis on landscape. As they became more familiar with good Chinese paintings, they began to incorporate more variety into their brushwork; with the paintings of Ike Taiga (1723–1776) and Yosa Buson (1716–1783), however, Nanga

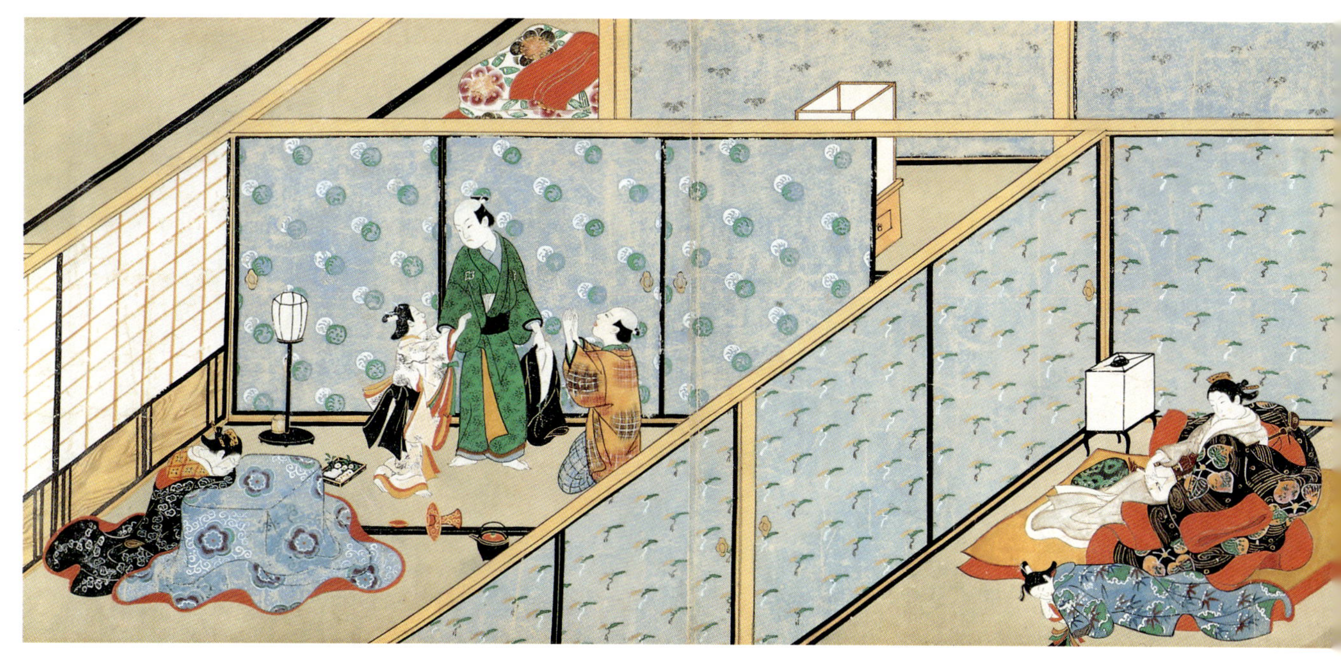

Plate 9 (detail) / No. 23
Scenes from the Yoshiwara District
attributed to Ōʼoka Michinobu
(fl. 1720–1740)
handscroll; ink, color, and gold
on paper
Edo period, 18th century
29.2 x 660.0 cm

took on a distinctly Japanese quality and was assimilated into the native painting tradition.

Taiga began his career as a professional artist rather than a true literatus, or scholar-amateur painter. (His wife, Gyokuran, also produced Nanga paintings.) A man of highly individual character, who blended a diversity of influences and techniques to create his own special style, he was well educated, although he did not undertake a formal study of Chinese literature. Much of his work relied on Chinese subject matter and brushwork, yet he also produced paintings on indigenous themes in a manner that demonstrated his knowledge of other schools.

The large painting entitled *The Four Accomplishments* (Fig. 12/No. 8) is Taiga's interpretation of one of the most famous of Chinese literary themes. It may be an early work and contains what are clearly awkward elements. The scholars depicted represent the so-called Four Scholarly Accomplishments: painting, music, calligraphy, and *go*, a chess-like board game. The relationship of their necks to their bodies is ambiguous, and the manner in which the shoulders of the literatus with his back to the viewer are depicted in heavy ink wash is rather crude. In spite of this, the picture is lively and entertaining. The viewer has the feeling that he is actually participating in the activities of these elderly gentlemen. The attention of the group, with the exception of the scholar hunched down behind the chessboard, is directed toward the calligrapher about to inscribe a poem onto his scroll. The figure of an impish young page, peering around the painting at his elders, adds a touch of humor and helps to make this a pleasing composition.

The Nanga school is also represented here by Hine Taizan (1813–1869), an artist of much later date. Taizan was born near Osaka, but he lived in Kyoto and practiced both calligraphy and painting. He appears to have had a rather self-important attitude and boisterous nature, although these characteristics are not usually reflected in his work. This hanging scroll, *Travelers in Cold Mountains* (Fig. 13/No. 15), derives its general style and motifs from Chinese scholar-painting, yet it is an intensely personal image. Snow-covered, twisted peaks sweep toward the sky like flames, and the placement of clusters of bare-limbed trees add to this sense of upward movement. Small figures of horsemen and travelers struggle upward, never down. In this work, Taizan attained the true goal of the literati painter: to express himself in an unmistakably individual way.

Another late Edo painter who worked in the Nanga manner was Watanabe Shōka (1835–1887). His father, Watanabe Kazan (1793–1841), painted in the Nanga style but also adopted Western rules of chiaroscuro and perspective. Shōka, an eclectic artist, appears to have inherited some of his father's talent for naturalism. His charming painting of *Cranes* (Plate 10, Frontispiece/No. 17) features delicate brushwork and a decorative use of color.

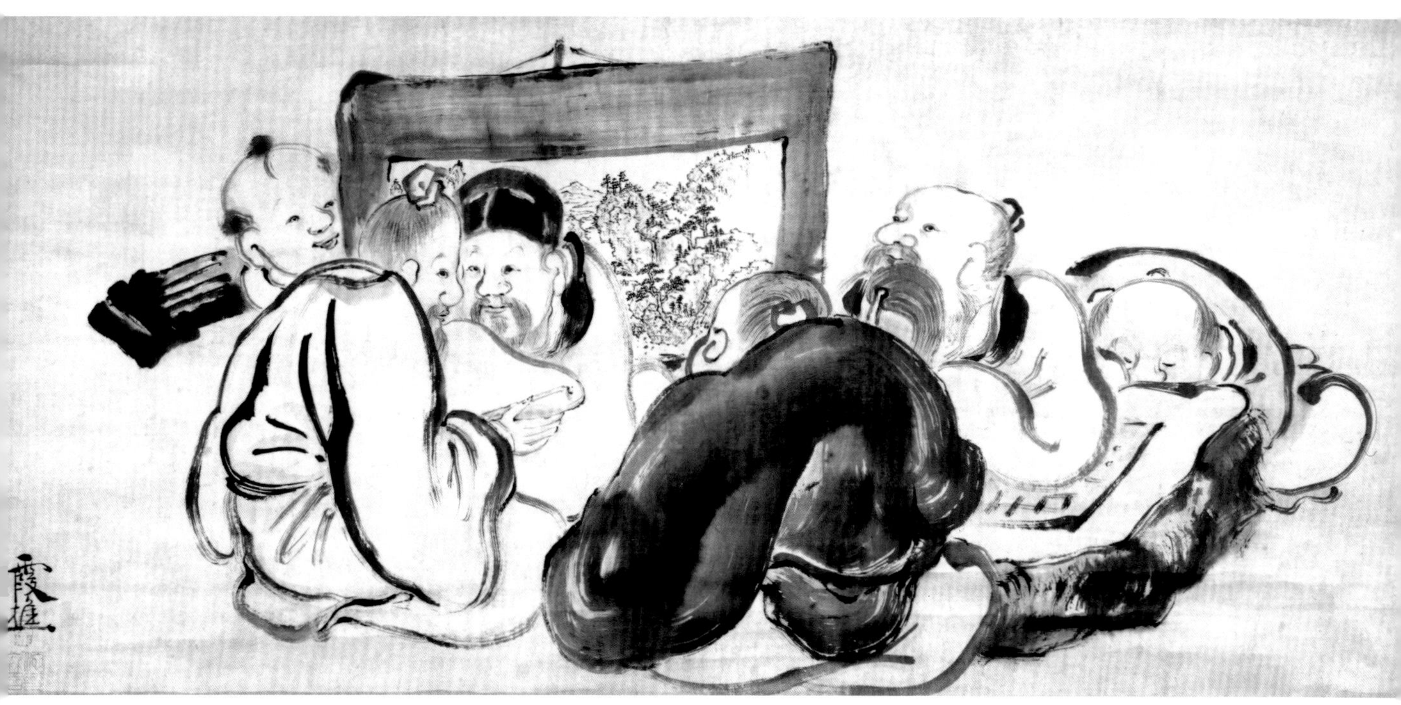

Fig. 12 / No. 8
The Four Accomplishments
by Ike Taiga (1723–1776)
Signature: Kashō
Seals: Sekitei, Ike Mumei in
hanging scroll; ink on paper
Edo period, 18th century
56.6 x 124.3 cm

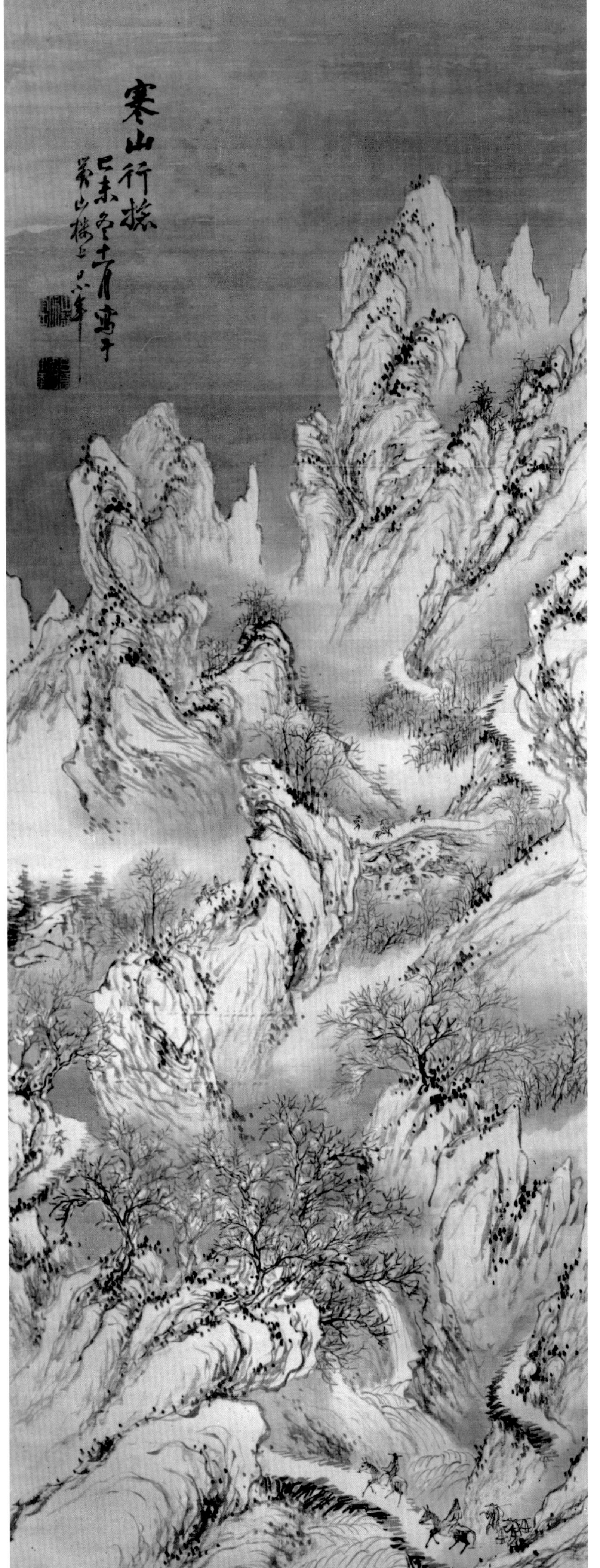

Fig. 13 / No. 15
Travelers in Cold Mountains
by Hine Taizan (1813–1869)
Signature: Shibi [1859]
fuyu jūichi gatsu
Taizan rōjō ni utsusu hi shōnen
Seals: Sansei ji taiko,
Hi Chōjo Shōnen
hanging scroll; ink and light
color on silk
Edo period, 19th century
137.2 x 51.5 cm

In the late Edo period, Maruyama Ōkyo (1733–1795) formed an important new school under his own name. It attracted many able pupils, among them the Nanga painter Matsumura Goshun (1753–1811). Goshun also founded a school, called Shijō after the Kyoto street on which he lived. The followers of these two masters are thus known collectively as members of the Maruyama-Shijō school. Ōkyo was one of the great figures in the history of Japanese painting. His eclectic training included study of the Tosa, Kano, and Rimpa traditions. An important influence upon his work came from Nagasaki, where the shogunate allowed Dutch and Chinese ships to bring their goods for trade. Here, as a result of contact with foreign books, scientific manuals, and other imported objects, Japanese artists became familiar with a different approach to visual reality. The Western emphasis on empirical study led them to an increased reliance on observation and the practice of making sketches from life.

Although he had studied Chinese painting early in his career, Ōkyo became an advocate of working from drawings taken from life. He also made intensive studies of the human figure, and produced "eyeglass pictures"—painted stereographs for use in a popular optical device—showing views of Chinese and Japanese landscapes executed in accordance with Western perspective. A popular and prolific painter, he executed many large-scale screens and wall paintings for temples and for the Imperial Palace in Kyoto. Even though Ōkyo and his followers adopted elements of Western-style realism, they never broke completely with native techniques and themes. Ōkyo captured the appearance of nature but retained the decorative gold backgrounds and compositions of the Kano and Tosa traditions in which he had been trained.

In *Goose and Reeds; Willows and Moon* (Fig. 14/No. 28), the pair of screens chosen for this exhibition, one may see how Ōkyo blended the disparate elements of realistic depiction, Chinese influence, and the indigenous Japanese sense of abstract design. This is particularly true in the right-hand screen, showing a single goose flying out to sea. The simple compositions in ink and light color on a pale background of gold wash evoke a sense of the loneliness and vastness of nature. The paintings exhibit compositional and thematic affinities with a four-fold screen by Ōkyo, in the Freer Gallery in Washington, which depicts two geese above a shore with waves emerging from a mist-filled distance. In both paintings, the point of view is placed low and the waves are seen close up, making the background space appear remarkably deep. Ōkyo's dated inscriptions appear on both screens. Inscribed on the back of the right screen is a statement of authentication by Ōshin (1790–1838), a grandson of Ōkyo, dated to the early spring of 1835.

Ōkyo's most inventive and eccentric pupil was Nagasawa Rōsetsu (1754–1799), who entered Ōkyo's school while in his early twenties. At first Rōsetsu painted in his master's immaculate and precise style,

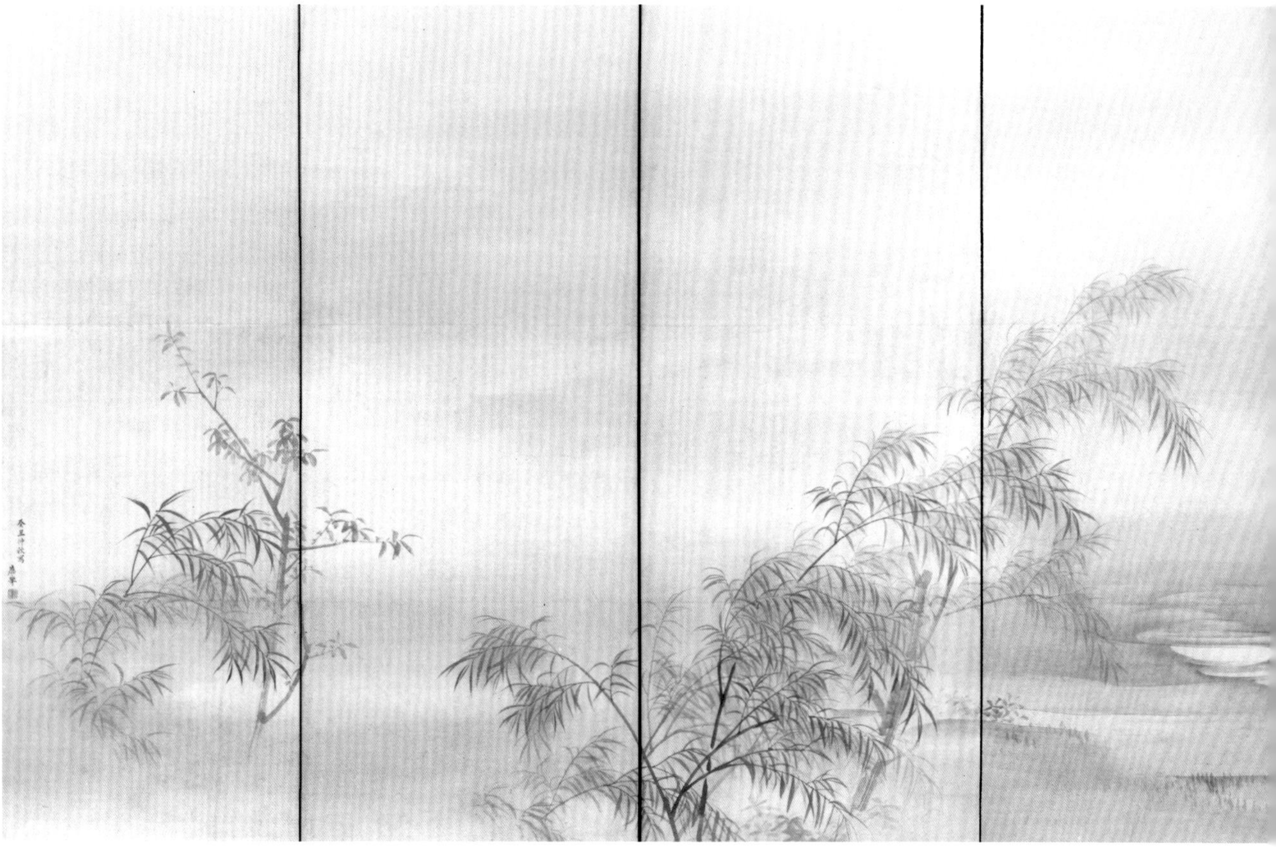

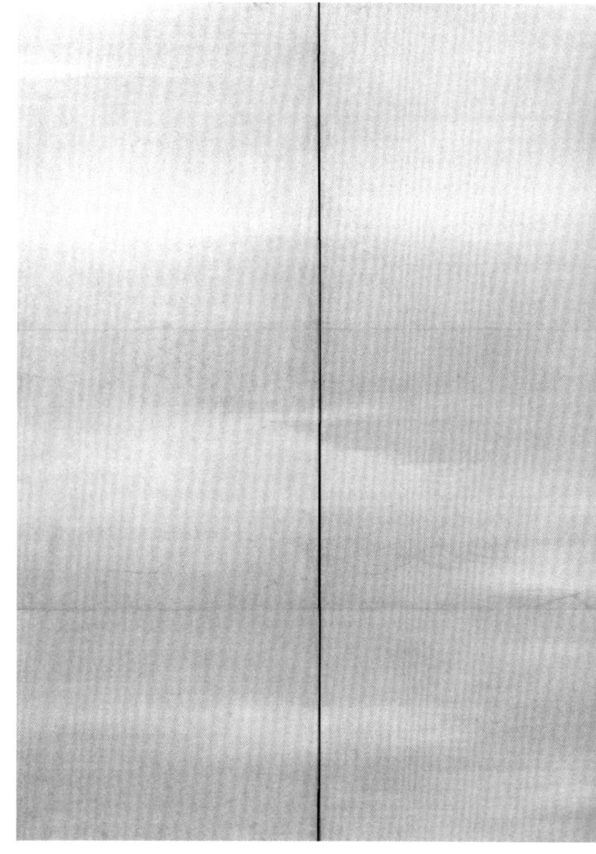

Fig. 14 / No. 28
Goose and Reeds; Willows and Moon
by Maruyama Ōkyo (1733–1795)
Signature: (left screen) Kichū [1793]
chūshū ni utsusu Ōkyo;
(right screen) An-ei Kōgo [1774]
kito ni utsusu Ōkyo
Seal: (left screen) Ōkyo-no-in;
(right screen) Ōkyo-no-in, Chūsen
pair of six-fold screens;
ink, light color, and gold wash on paper
Edo period, 18th century
153.9 x 354.2 cm (left screen);
153.9 x 353.8 cm (right screen)

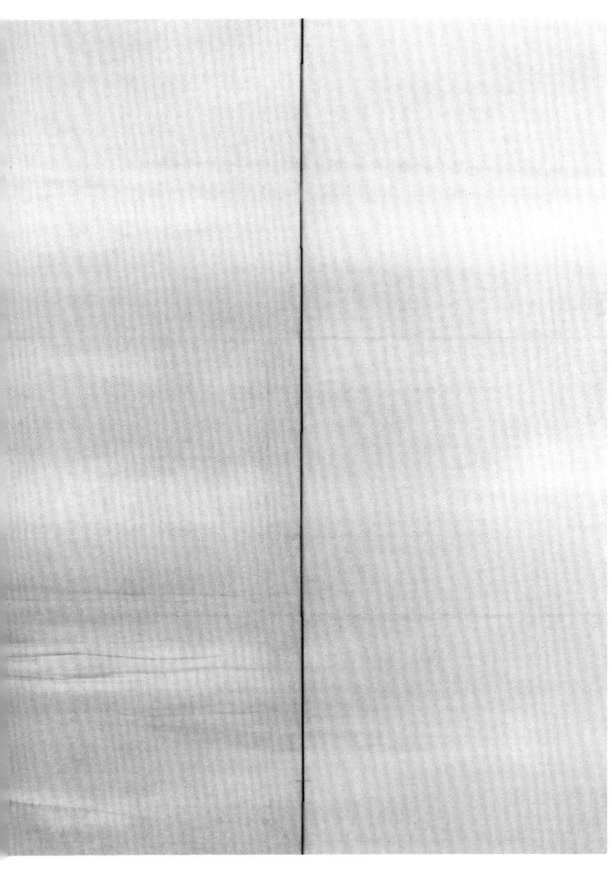

but differences soon began to appear. His work moved away from Ōkyo's quiet models as he attempted to express movement and emotion rather than perfection. Rōsetsu also avoided the brilliant colors Ōkyo often used, preferring lighter shades to produce mysterious, sensuous effects. Unlike his teacher, Rōsetsu was not content to satisfy his clients by producing calm, visually pleasing pictures. He wished to surprise, even to shock. He must not have been completely happy in the rigidly controlled society of eighteenth-century Edo. He drank heavily, in part, perhaps, to express his displeasure with authority. In his late thirties, he worked for the Kishimoto family, for whom he painted a number of masterpieces. The Kishimotos were wealthy merchants, patrons of scholars and artists (including Ōkyo). They are still much involved with art matters today. During the late Edo period, they also sold *sake*, and one of the present-day Kishimotos once told me that Rōsetsu often paid his delinquent bills for this commodity by presenting the family with paintings.

For subject matter, Rōsetsu frequently utilized Chinese themes having to do with drinking. His painting *Chinese Officials and Scholars with Attendants* (Fig. 15/No. 10) seems to celebrate his sense of spiritual and artistic freedom, combined with a strong desire to make fun of stuffy authoritative figures. Chinese art has produced numerous works in which dignified officials and scholars engage in worthy artistic or literary pursuits while indulging in a little wine or tea, prepared for them by servants. The staid Confucian gentlemen depicted in such images are generally the epitome of propriety as they carefully examine picture scrolls or discuss weighty philosphical matters. What a contrast they make to the figures in Rōsetsu's unruly but highly entertaining composition.

In *Chinese Officials*, the eye is first caught by the old man in the foreground, to whom attendants present a painting. It is difficult to determine whether he is contemplating the painting or sleeping. He sits in the midst of so much confused activity that concentration must be impossible. With the exception of a man in the central area of the composition, who looks into the distance as he applies his brush to paper, most of the officials appear to be lining up for a drink. At least one scholar is well into his cups; another is clearly a two-fisted drinker. Many servants are present to brew tea and serve wine to the scholars and officials. Two attendants prepare ink under the table of an artist (or calligrapher). Two small Ōkyo-style dogs, lying in the middle of the chaos, provide an amusing touch.

A curious element is the group of straining laborers pulling a cart, which may be filled with books. In the background, another, smaller group of scholars is gathered around tables laden with wine pots. Two cranes—birds often shown in the company of scholar-gentlemen—fly high overhead. Perhaps they have been frightened away by the proceedings.

It is difficult to know exactly what Rōsetsu had in mind when he

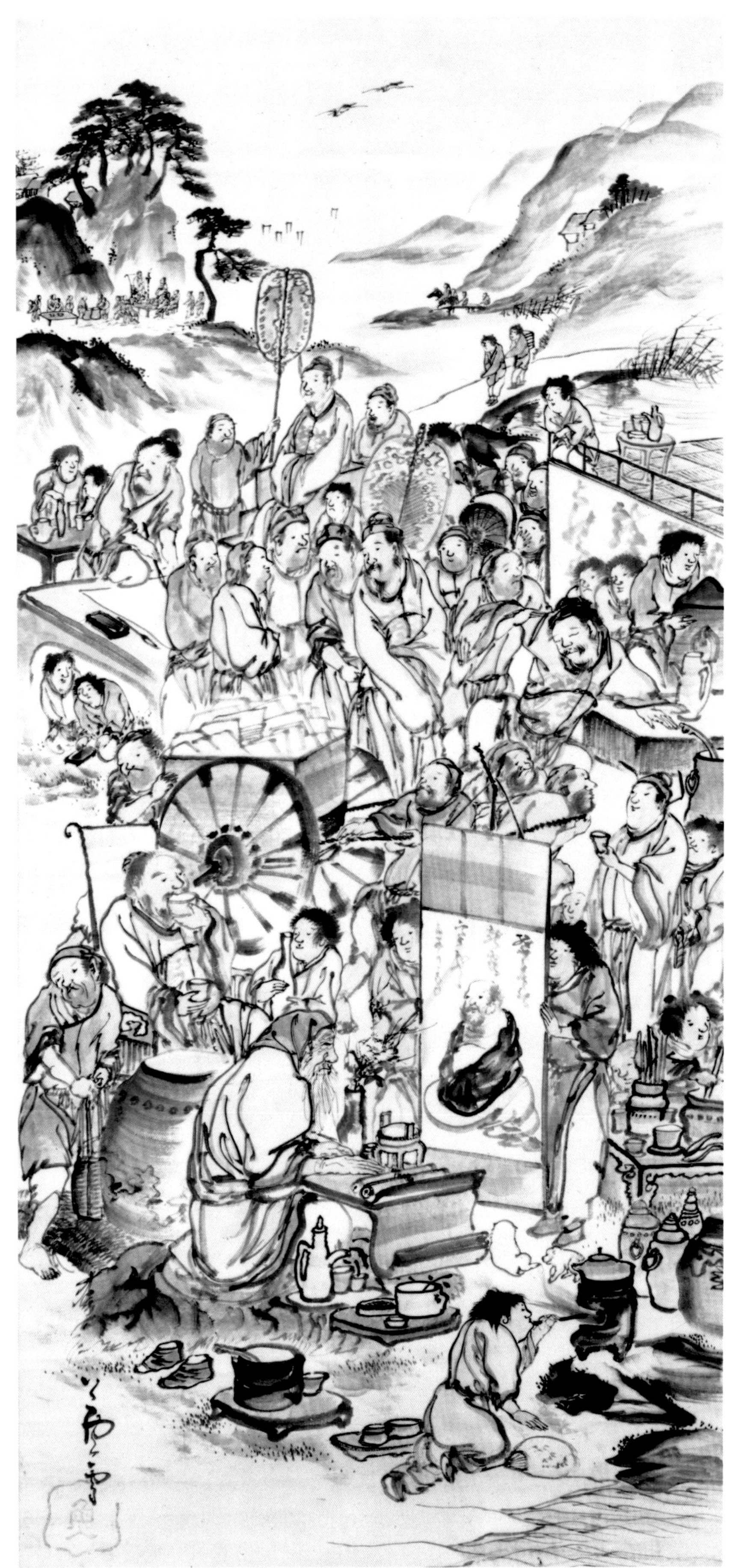

Fig. 15 / No. 10
Chinese Officials and Scholars with Attendants
attributed to Nagasawa Rōsetsu (1754–1799)
Signature: Rōsetsu
Seal: Gyo
hanging scroll; ink and light color on paper
Edo period, 18th century
131.1 x 60.1 cm

painted this hanging scroll. The Chinese had their own, more sedate variety of paintings celebrating the joys of wine, as well as the more formal pleasures of literary and artistic gatherings. Perhaps Rōsetsu combined an assortment of Chinese themes to express his individualistic, untrammeled view of life and art.

Before concluding a discussion of Edo-period painting, it is necessary to mention again the so-called *namban* (southern barbarian) art, produced following the arrival of Westerners in Japan. Unfortunately, space does not permit me to deal with the first wave of this foreign influence. The Portuguese first landed on a small island south of Kyūshū in 1543 and, by 1571, a brisk and profitable trade with Japan had been established. In 1642, however, the Portuguese and other Europeans were expelled, due to suspicions that they hoped to conquer Japan through, among other things, the promulgation of Christianity. The Dutch (known among the Japanese as *kōmō*, or "redheads") showed little interest in religious proselytizing and were allowed to maintain limited contact with Japan. *Dutch Lady with Attendant* (Plate 11/No. 11) is an attempt made by a late-eighteenth-century artist to depict one of the foreigners who came to the man-made island of Dejima in Nagasaki harbor—the area to which they were restricted.

So completely had the efficient Edo government stamped out remnants of Christianity and European cultural influence that most Edo-period artists had little access to Western-style painting until they began to study books and pictures brought by the Dutch in their seventeenth- and eighteenth-century trading expeditions. This painting of a Dutch woman, her attendant, and dog is difficult to classify. It has a charming naïveté, and exhibits native Japanese characteristics in the delineation of the pine trees and the use of strong, flat areas of color; however, it also contains attempts at shading to convey a sense of three-dimensionality.

The painting may be a copy of a work by the Nagasaki-based painter Kawahara Keiga (1786–?). Keiga was a disciple of Ishizaki Yūshi (1768–1846), an artist who held the position of official appraiser of foreign pictures. Yūshi chronicled the artifacts and activities of the Dutch residing on Dejima until his retirement in 1832. His sponsorship gave Keiga access to the Dejima compound and a proximity to its inhabitants such as was enjoyed by few Japanese. He could observe the foreigners first-hand, and also examine Western pictures. By the age of thirty, he had gained some renown as a portrait painter through his many pictures of Dutch traders. He is said to have developed a new method of looking at his subjects which was an interesting amalgam of Western and Japanese traditions.

Among the foreigners Keiga painted was a certain Captain Jan Cock Blomhoff (1779–1853), who, in defiance of Japanese law, brought his wife, Titia, his infant son, Johannes, and the child's

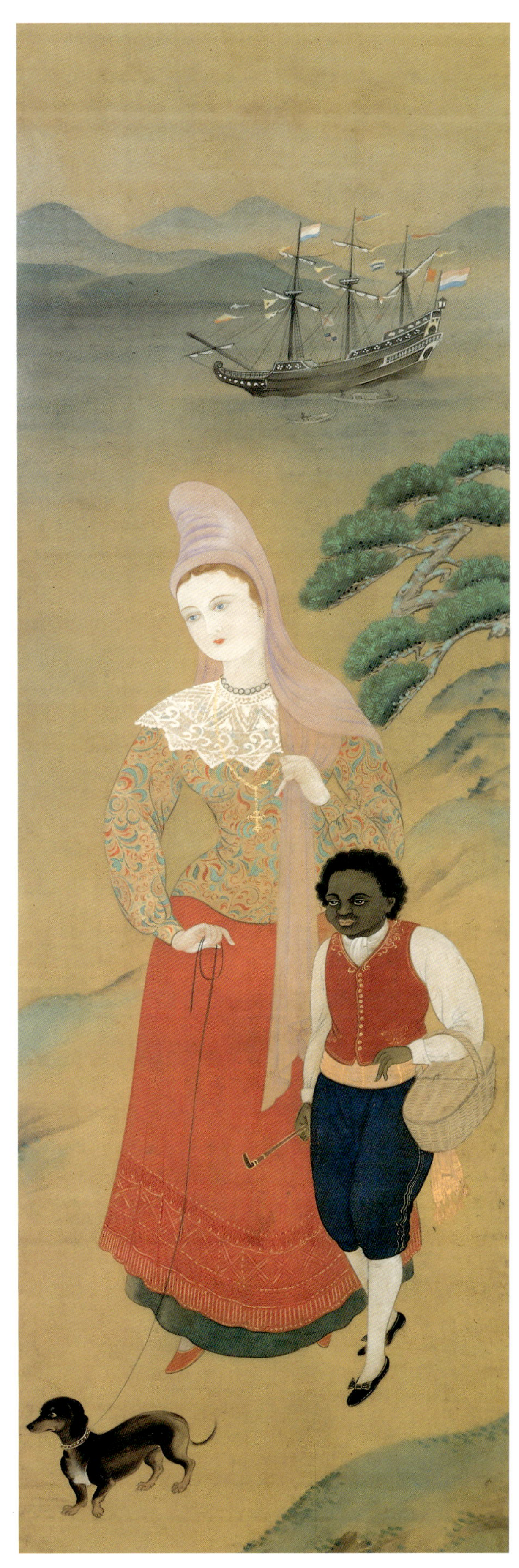

Plate 11 / No. 11
Dutch Lady with Attendant
hanging scroll;
color and ink on silk
Edo period, late 18th century
106.5 x 34.5 cm

nursemaid, Petronella Munts, to Dejima. Within months of their arrival, Titia, her baby, and the nurse were sent back to Europe on the first available ship. Blomhoff was obliged to remain behind until 1823, to serve out his term as principal executive officer of the Dutch East India Company.

The visit of Blomhoff's family made a tremendous impression on the Japanese, who had never before seen a Western woman. For decades after their departure, the print shops of Nagasaki continued to produce pictures of the female foreigners. Both Yūshi and Keiga did paintings of the Blomhoff family. These works depicted various groupings of the members of the captain's household: Blomhoff himself, his wife, baby, the nursemaid, and the Indonesian servant, Maraty. One portrait, currently housed in the Nagasaki Prefectural Museum, depicts Titia and the dark-skinned Maraty, and bears two of Keiga's most commonly used seals. In this work, probably based on direct observation, Titia's hair is partially covered by a lace headdress, and she is distinguished by her bright blue eyes, pale skin, and long nose. At the same time, she is generalized into a type of figure employed by many Japanese artists when depicting foreigners. Generalization also appears in the rendition of Maraty, who is shown as being quite short with near-black skin, flaring nostrils, and lustrous black eyes (Michael L. Browne, "Portraits of Foreigners by Kawahara Keiga," 1985, p. 33). This painting bears some similarities to the work exhibited here.

The last paintings to be considered in this exhibition, *Amanoiwato* and *The Death of Śākyamuni Buddha* (Plates 12 and 13/No. 18), are a pair by Kōno Bairei (1844–1895), an artist of the Meiji period (1868–1912). Although he was a central figure, both as teacher and artist, in the Maruyama-Shijō school, Bairei often worked in the literati mode. He was a man of his times, caught up in the stresses and strains of the era during which Japan propelled itself into the modern age. In the Meiji era, education was of the utmost importance, and Bairei, a student of literature and Confucianism, was deeply involved in educational work. He started an art school, promoted many painters, and became a member of the Art Committee of the Imperial Household. A cultured and philosophical man, he was probably also aware of the new controversy concerning Buddhism and Shinto.

In their efforts to modernize Japan, leaders of the Meiji period realized the need for a strong, centralized government. In their view, none of the traditional religions—Shinto, Buddhism, or Confucianism—could serve as a spiritual axis to unite the nation. They needed a new form of religion: a national entity around which people could rally. Thus, they created State Shinto, with the emperor as its sacred focus. In order to institute this "new" faith, "the government had to transform traditional Shinto, and this meant the rejection of the historic amalgamation of Shinto and Buddhism" (Kitagawa, *On*

Understanding Japanese Religion, 1987, p. 214). Measures undertaken to separate Buddhism from Shinto precipitated a popular anti-Buddhist movement; this resulted in the loss of government stipends and other means of support for the Buddhists.

It is obvious from the subject matter of this pair of paintings that Bairei had strong feelings about the government's religious reform. It is impossible to know for certain where his true religious affiliations lay, but one may hazard a reasonable guess from clues provided by these two paintings. Bairei chose to illustrate two climactic moments from Shinto and Buddhist legends. In *Amanoiwato (The Rock Door of Heaven)*, the painting on the right, he depicts an event involving the sun goddess Amaterasu. The tale is derived from the rich mythology of creation recorded in two eighth-century works, the *Kojiki (Record of Ancient Matters)* and the *Nihon Shoki (Chronicles of Japan)*. The sun goddess, appointed to rule over the plain of high heaven, has hidden herself in a cave because of her displeasure at the boorish behavior of her brother, Susanō-ō. After Amaterasu goes into seclusion, the earth is plunged into darkness. To entice her out, the other deities organize a program of wild entertainment. This includes a dance performed by Ama no Uzame (Terrible Female of Heaven), who brandishes a spear in one hand. A cock is placed in front of the cave to mark the beginning of the festivities. When the curious sun goddess peers out, she is seized by one of the waiting deities and pulled into the open, thereby restoring light to the world.

In his portrayal of this mythical event, Bairei follows the legend closely and is highly attentive to the smallest detail. Besides the rooster, he depicts a *sakaki* tree, its branches laden with jewels, a mirror, and offerings, all of which are mentioned in the *Kojiki*. He even paints the *sakaki* leaves worn by the dancer, the fire she has kindled, and the tub she has placed, bottom upward, to dance on. The work is executed in shades of light ink, with touches of gold on ornaments, musical instruments, headgear, and weapons, and flesh tones on faces and hands. Gold also appears on the hanging strips around the sacred mirror in the *sakaki* tree. A subtle wash of gold represents sunbeams emanating from the crack between the great boulders that close off the sun goddess' cave, indicating that she is peering out at the proceedings as two gods rush forward to pull her out. In the landscape, Bairei uses the Chinese convention of ink dots to denote vegetation.

The second painting in Bairei's diptych illustrates the *Nehan*, or final moment in the life of the historical Buddha, Śākyamuni (*Shaka*, in Japanese). It embodies the ultimate quest of all Buddhists, as it signifies not death but release from the dreaded cycle of birth and rebirth. The Buddha lies on his right side with his right arm bent, on a couch in a forest of *śāla* trees at Kushinogana, by the bank of the Ajiravati River in India. His followers rush to his side from the four corners of the world and various species of animals also gather

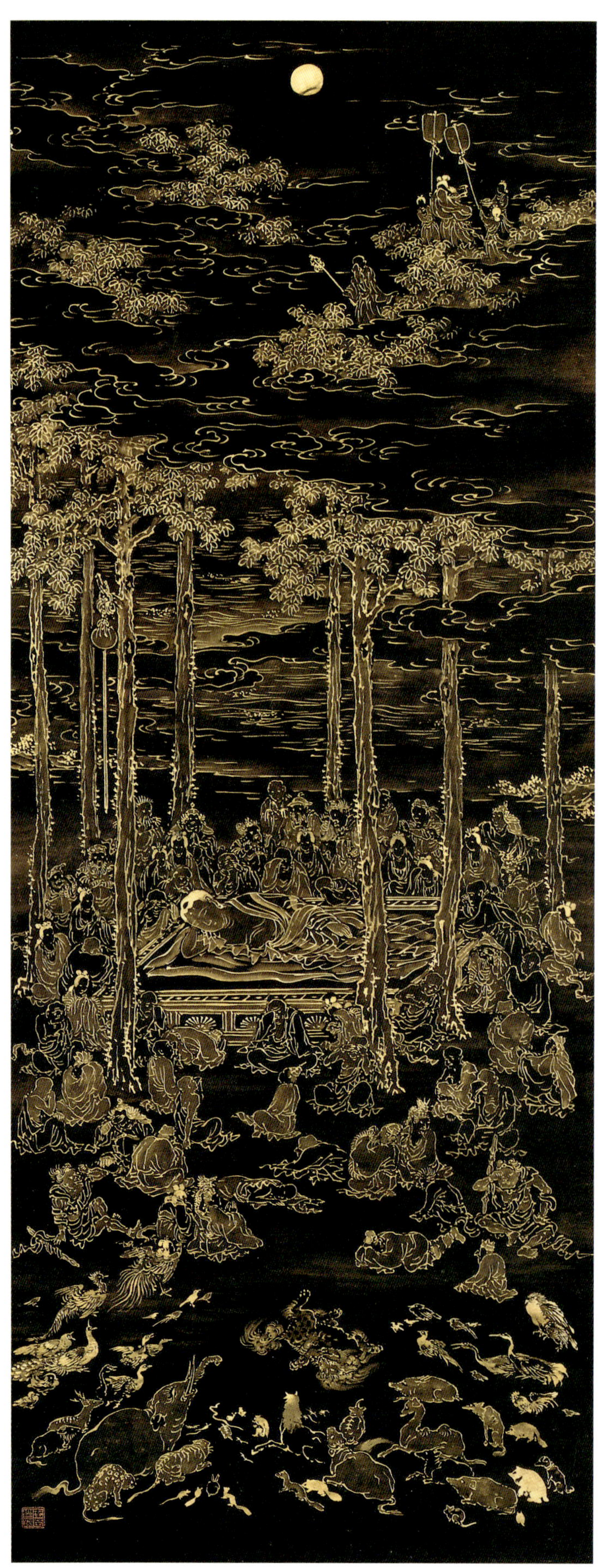

Plates 12, 13 / No. 18
Amanoiwato and
The Death of Śākyamuni
Buddha
by Kōno Bairei (1844–1895)
Seal: (each painting) Kōno hōin
pair of hanging scrolls;
ink, color, and gold on silk
Meiji period, 19th century
70.5 x 27.0 cm (each scroll)

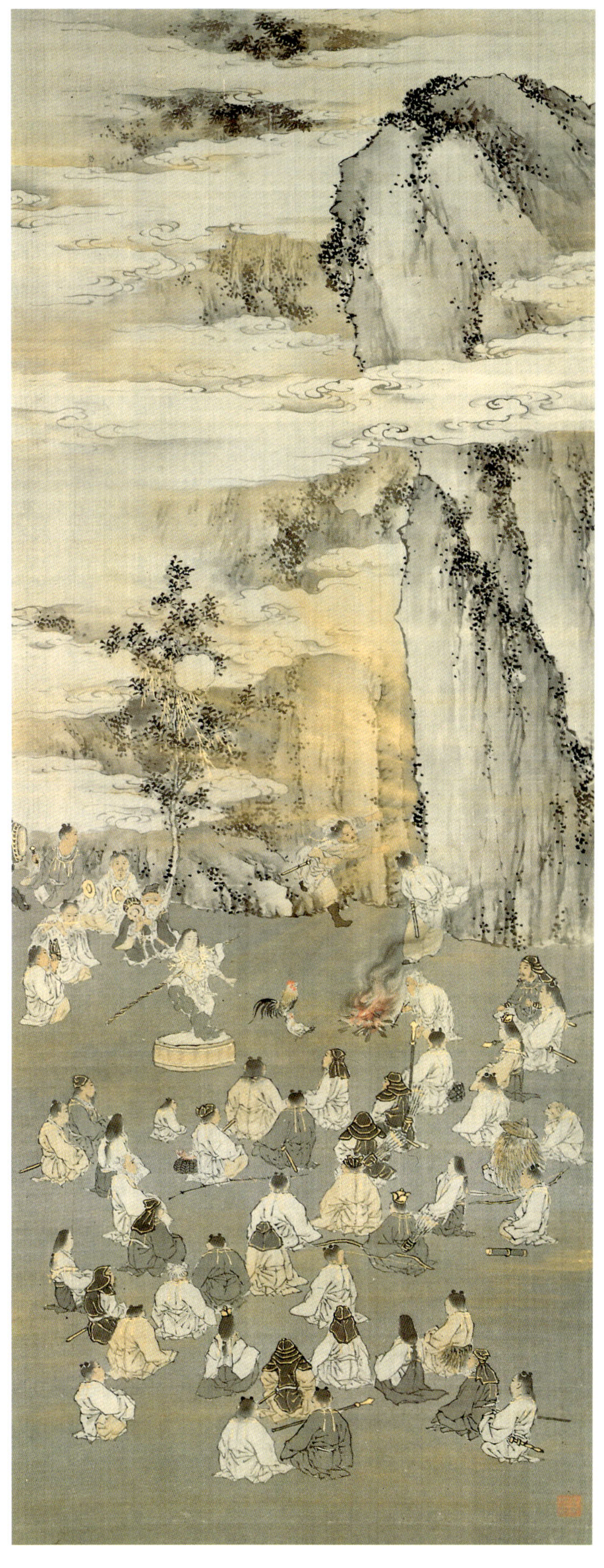

nearby to witness the last moments of the Buddha's life on earth.

The earliest extant rendition of this subject in Japan dates to about 710, and basic iconography of the *Nehan* remained relatively constant over the centuries. In Bairei's work, bodhisattvas, monks, devas (fierce guardians), and lay followers are gathered around the Buddha's couch. Above the clouds rise the branches of eight *śāla* trees. The Buddha's golden staff and alms bowl wrapped in a cloth hang from one of the lower branches. In the upper right-hand corner, Queen Maya, mother of Śākyamuni, and an attendant, follow the monk Aniruddha, the disciple sent to report the news of the Buddha's passing.

While the painting follows traditional *Nehan* iconography, it differs in palette and style from the colorful versions usually seen in temples. In this small delicate work, executed in gold on dark-blue silk, Bairei has gone back to the sutra-painting technique of the Heian period. However, the brushwork he employs is different from that used by Heian artists. Instead of a smooth, continuous line of even width, he uses a frequently broken stroke which varies in thickness. The drawing is free and lively, more naturalistic than those found in earlier types of Buddhist painting. In this painting and its companion piece, he displays both his Nanga and his Maruyama-Shijō training.

Exactly what was Bairei trying to express with regard to Shinto and Buddhism? In particular, what was his attitude toward the Meiji government's policy of State Shinto, and the subsequent downgrading of Buddhism? Bairei chose to illustrate episodes from both Shinto and Buddhist legend: events of as much importance to each of these religions as the birth of Christ and his crucifixion have been to Christianity. He executed the paintings in this diptych with exquisite care, but each in a different style. The Shinto image exhibits a Meiji-period aesthetic, combining ancient Japanese traditions with techniques borrowed from the West. Realistic and alive, it is a perfect vehicle to represent a dramatic, epic beginning for the nation—a realization of the ancient myth of the ancestress of the emperor. It was Amaterasu who bestowed the sacred regalia—a mirror, a sword, and a curved jewel—upon her grandson Ninigi before sending him to earth to rule over the islands of Japan. In historical times, this group of three items was used exclusively as a token of the imperial family's right to reign.

It is clear that Bairei took pleasure in the sun goddess myth, which had rarely, if ever, been illustrated before. Perhaps he wished to help Meiji leaders establish the legend's historical validity. In the light of the other half of the diptych, however, it does not appear that he meant to promote Shinto at the expense of Buddhism. In the *Nehan* scene, he treated the Buddha with great respect, but chose to combine his animated, naturalistic painting style with a palette reminiscent of much earlier Buddhist images. Buddhism is no longer in its heyday, he seems to say; but it deserves to be honored as something venerable and beautiful. In these paintings, Bairei has brought together several traditions and elements of Japanese art and culture. This is therefore an appropriate point at which to leave the painting medium and turn briefly to lacquer and the ceramic arts.

Lacquer and Ceramics: Objects of Function and Beauty

Japanese lacquerware has always had tremendous appeal for me. Even the most simple, undecorated pieces are remarkably beautiful. Used for many different kinds of household objects as a protective coating, lacquer is a useful as well as visually pleasing material. It is in essence a natural sealant, which, when applied to a surface, hardens and creates a water-impermeable outer layer. The technique of treating objects with many layers of refined sap from the lacquer tree *(rhus verniciflua)* is time-consuming, laborious, and complicated. Tapped almost like maple syrup, the lacquer is clarified before being brushed over a supporting body, usually wood, basketwork, or textile. Numerous methods can be used to decorate lacquerworks. Certain pigments, chemically compatible with raw lacquer, can be added to produce colors. Red and black were the most common colors of early lacquer, but yellow, green, and brown were also used. The Edo period produced an even greater variety in lacquer-decorating technique. Lacquer could be carved, incised, or inlaid with metals, mother-of-pearl, and other materials. The eighteenth-century writing box (Plate 14/No. 50) in this exhibition is a handsome example of inlaid lacquer. Its cover design of an arched bridge and waves is rendered in two different types of inlay. Glistening mother-of-pearl was used for the pilings and railings, while metal was applied for the walkway. Repeated wave patterns below were executed in gold *maki-e* (sprinkled gold powder). The image is reminiscent of Rimpa design in its decorative treatment of simple motifs. It may also be a reference to Uji Bridge, a site made famous by classical poetry and narrative literature, which frequently appeared as the subject of Edo-period screens and lacquerware. In contrast to the schematized design of the lid, the interior is decorated with a more naturalistic scene of geese, reeds, and water.

The term *maki-e*, literally "sprinkled picture," encompasses a variety of techniques employing gold or silver powder, or particles, sprinkled on areas of wet lacquer to create a design. The metal powders adhere to the lacquer as it hardens. *Maki-e* was the principal method of decoration for high-quality lacquers during Heian times, and each period produced new innovations.

Lacquers often feature motifs drawn from literature. The stacked boxes with a design of the Thirty-six Immortal Poets (see Fig. 4/No. 52), discussed earlier, recall the classical era in their depiction of the poets in gold against a black background. The poets are rendered in a method known as *chinkinbori* (shallow-incised lacquer). Such

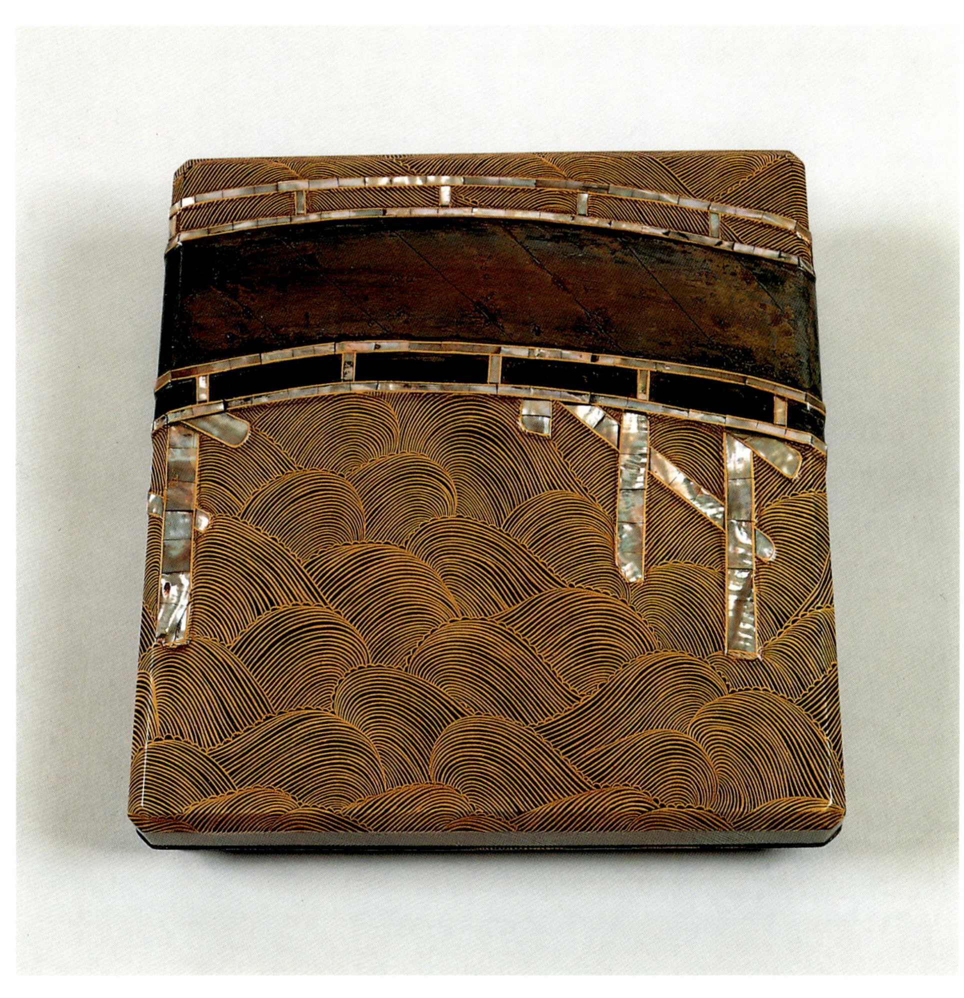

Plate 14 / No. 50
Writing box with design of
bridge and waves
black lacquer with sprinkled gold,
metal and shell inlay
Edo period, 18th century
H: 4.3 cm, L: 22.4 cm, W: 21.0 cm

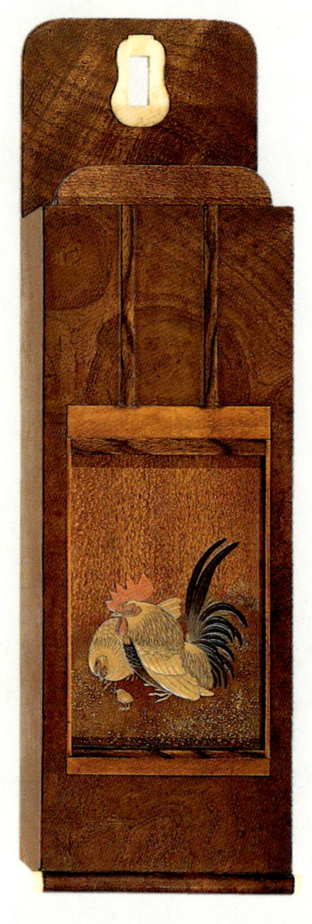

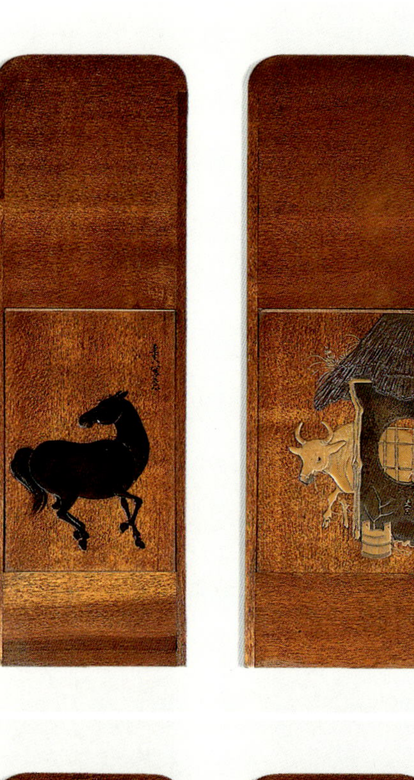

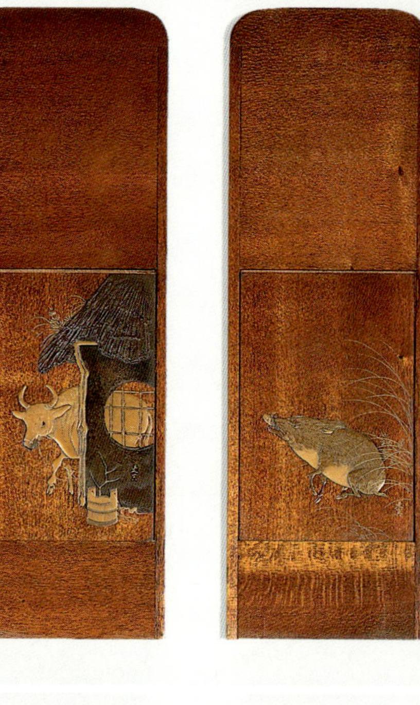

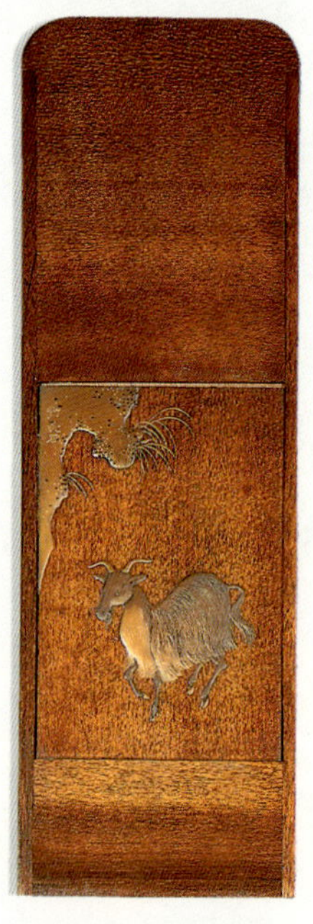

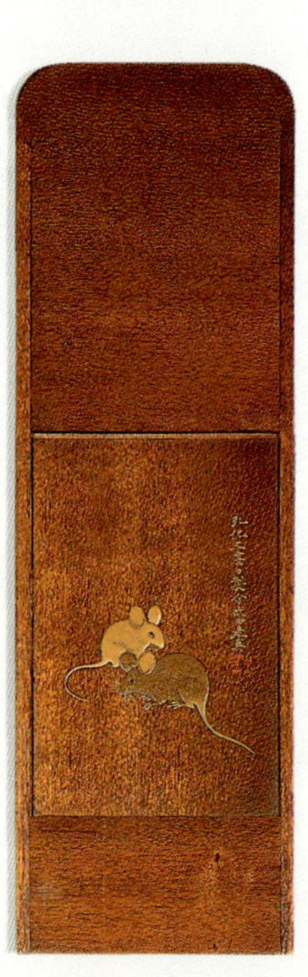

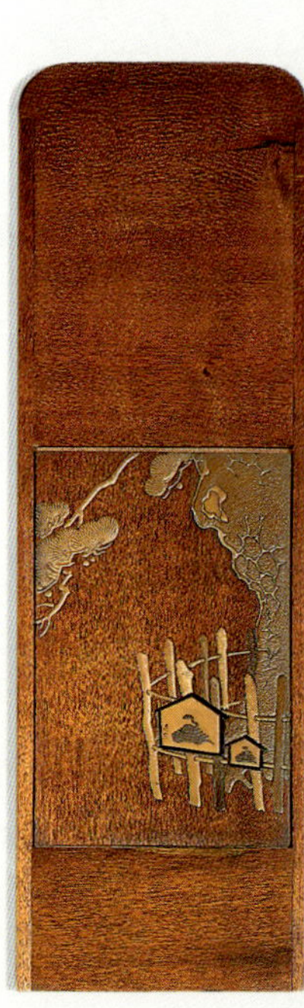

Plate 15 / No. 53
Zodiac calendar with holder in the shape of a hanging scroll
by Shibata Zeshin (1807–1891)
Signature: Kōka san [1846] natsu hi sei reiya ta Zeshin
Seal: Koma

wood with lacquer, shell, and sprinkled gold and silver
19th century
H: 25.7 cm, L: 7.8 cm, W: 4.3 cm (holder)
L: 19.9 cm, W: 6.2 cm (each plaque)

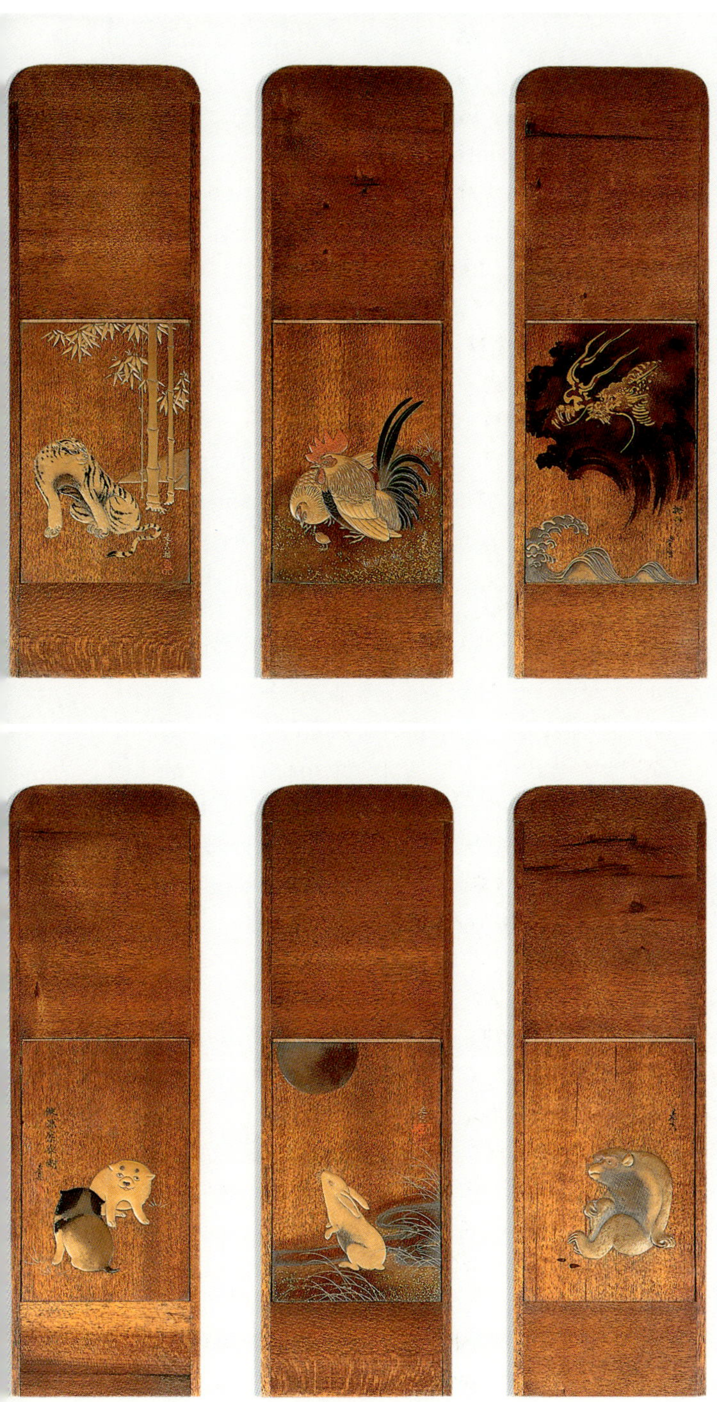

incised designs are usually filled with gold powder to contrast with the dark background.

The zodiac calendar (Plate 15/No. 53) by Shibata Zeshin (1807–1891) is a particularly charming, decorative piece. Zeshin was an outstanding artist and master of the lacquerware craft. Although he studied lacquer-making for eight years, he also studied painting with the Maruyama-Shijō school and produced a number of dramatic hanging scrolls and screens. In his later years he added the unusual technique of *urushi-e* (lacquer painting) to his repertoire. Inspired by Western oil painting, he created works that won prizes at expositions in Europe and America, and became involved in the decoration of the Imperial Palace in Tokyo. Zeshin used subtle textural contrasts on black, brown, or green backgrounds and found inspiration for his designs in both the Rimpa and Shijō schools.

With this work, Zeshin displays his technical virtuosity and his capacity for imaginative design. The calendar consists of six plaques, each side of which features a single symbol from the traditional Chinese zodiac. The plaque holder cleverly mimics the shape and format of a hanging scroll, even to the detail of the ivory roller ends. The symbolic creatures, representative of the twelve-year and twelve-month cycles, are paired off (front-to-back on the plaques) as follows: Rat and Ox, Tiger and Rabbit, Dragon and Snake, Horse and Ram, Monkey and Cock, Dog and Boar.

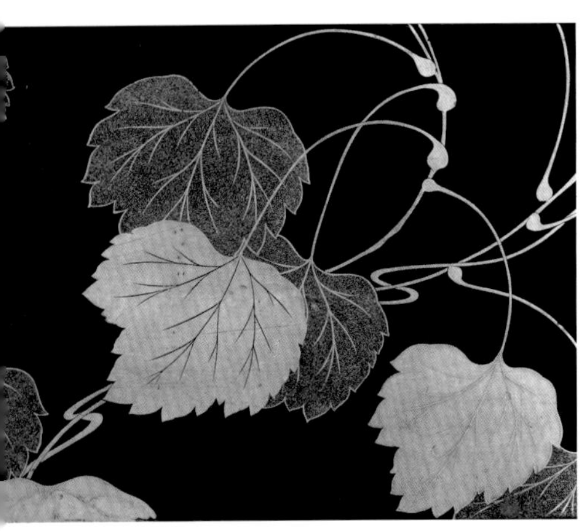

The principal lacquer technique used by Zeshin is *takamaki-e* (raised sprinkled design). In this method, the pictorial elements are raised above the surface by one or more foundation layers to which a thickening agent, usually clay or charcoal powder, has been added. Gold or silver powders are sprinkled over the moist design, a protective coat of clear lacquer is brushed on as a top coat, and the piece (once hardened) is polished. These signed plaques feature the gold and silver powders of traditional *maki-e* technique, with two exceptions. The first is the dragon plaque, which is decorated with a painting in lacquer; here, in addition to his own signature, Zeshin has inscribed Kano Tan'yū's name to indicate that he is painting in the style of the Kano master. The second exception is the horse plaque, which is executed in raised, polished black lacquer. In the plaque representing the dog, Zeshin has depicted two fat puppies with an inscription that reads: "copied after an original by Ōkyo." In the inscription for the rat plaque, Zeshin has included a cyclical date corresponding to the year 1849. Touches of red (on the cock's comb and on an occasional seal) also appear. Some of the writing and seals on these plaques are so minute that a magnifying glass is required to read them.

Two pieces in this exhibition, a tea caddy with design of "Autumn Fire" (Plate 16/No. 54) and another decorated with a cloud pattern (Plate 17/No. 55), are the work of a Kyoto-based husband-and-wife team still actively engaged in creating beautiful objects. Suzuki

No. 48
Cabinet with grapevine design (detail)
black lacquer with sprinkled gold
Edo period, 17th century
H: 19.1 cm, L: 30.2 cm, W: 16 cm

Mutsumi (b. 1941) is a son of the well-known lacquer artist Hyōsaku (1874–1942). He designs and creates the shapes of the pieces, and lacquers them in black or red. His wife, Suzuki Misako (b. 1945), sometimes decorates their surfaces. Both are highly adept at using traditional motifs and lacquering methods in new ways. The shapes and designs they employ give a sense of freshness and inspiration but are never jarring, as many contemporary designs applied to lacquerware can be. They also take great pains with their materials. The gold and silver powder used for Mrs. Suzuki's *maki-e* designs are acquired in twenty different grades, ranging in fineness from dust to coarse chips. Wood for the cores—preferably zelkova, cedar, or cypress— must be properly aged so that the finished product will not warp or crack.

Suzuki Misako uses a variety of techniques to decorate her husband's objects, and particularly excels in the use of *maki-e*. On the "Cloud Design" caddy, silver and gold powder has been sprinkled on a red background to form a traditional curling cloud pattern. On the "Autumn Fire" caddy she has painted a naturalistic flame design in red lacquer against a black background. The burning golden leaves, executed in *maki-e*, are raised slightly above the surface of the piece.

In studying contemporary lacquerwares, such as the Suzuki tea caddies, one becomes aware of how large a role *chanoyu* (the tea ceremony) plays in determining the nature of crafts produced in Japan. The history of tea in that country can be traced back to the introduction of Chinese culture in the sixth century, although the beverage received relatively little notice until the arrival of Zen Buddhism in the thirteenth century. At first, Zen monks used tea as a stimulant, to prevent them from falling asleep during their lengthy meditation sessions. By the fourteenth and fifteenth centuries, however, tea connoisseurship had gained popularity among the more educated *daimyo* and other members of elite society; as a result it became fashionable to collect tea ceramics and tea utensils imported from China. By the late Muromachi period, *chanoyu* began to take on a distinctly Japanized form, which featured the use of native ceramics as opposed to Chinese ware. The tea bowls and water jars preferred by such tea masters as Sen no Rikyū (1522–1591) were generally plain, unpretentious pieces, appreciated for their simplicity, naturalness, and even flaws and imperfections.

Enthusiasm for *chanoyu* was transmitted to the shoguns of the fifteenth and sixteenth centuries, and then to the warlords and rulers of the Momoyama and Edo periods. One of these military leaders, Toyotomi Hideyoshi (1536–1598), failed in his two attempts to conquer Korea, yet he did return home with Korean potters "kidnaped" to improve Japan's kiln technology and produce ceramics, including tea wares. Many masters of the art of tea flourished, and their descendants and heirs established different "schools" of tea. The two most important of these schools—Ura Senke, which represents the

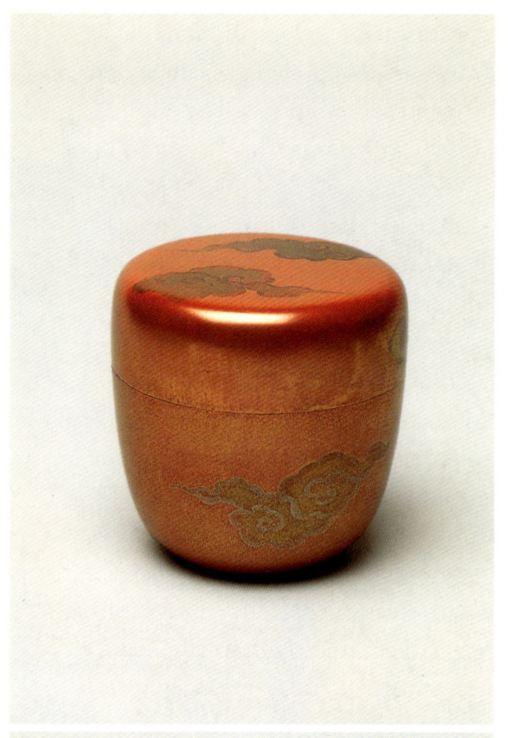

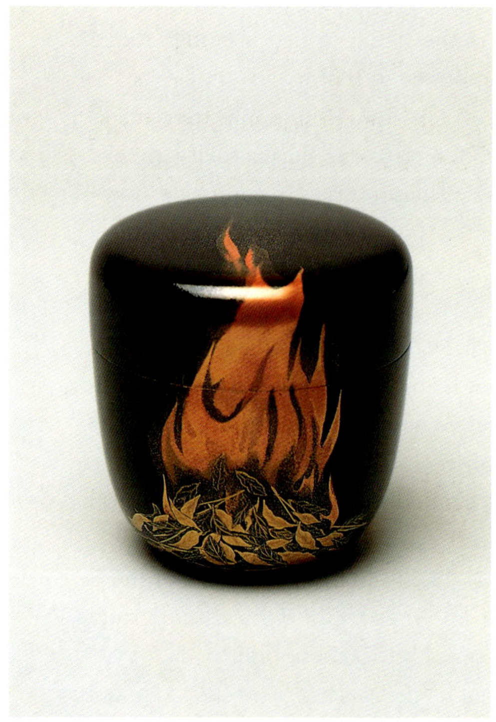

Plate 17 / No. 55
Tea caddy with "Cloud Design"
by Suzuki Mutsumi (b. 1941)
and Suzuki Misako (b. 1945)
red lacquer with
sprinkled gold and silver
20th century
H: 7.8 cm, Diam: 7.3 cm

Plate 16 / No. 54
Tea caddy with "Autumn Fire Design"
by Suzuki Mutsumi (b. 1941)
and Suzuki Misako (b. 1945)
black and red lacquer with
sprinkled gold
20th century
H: 7.7 cm, Diam: 7.2 cm

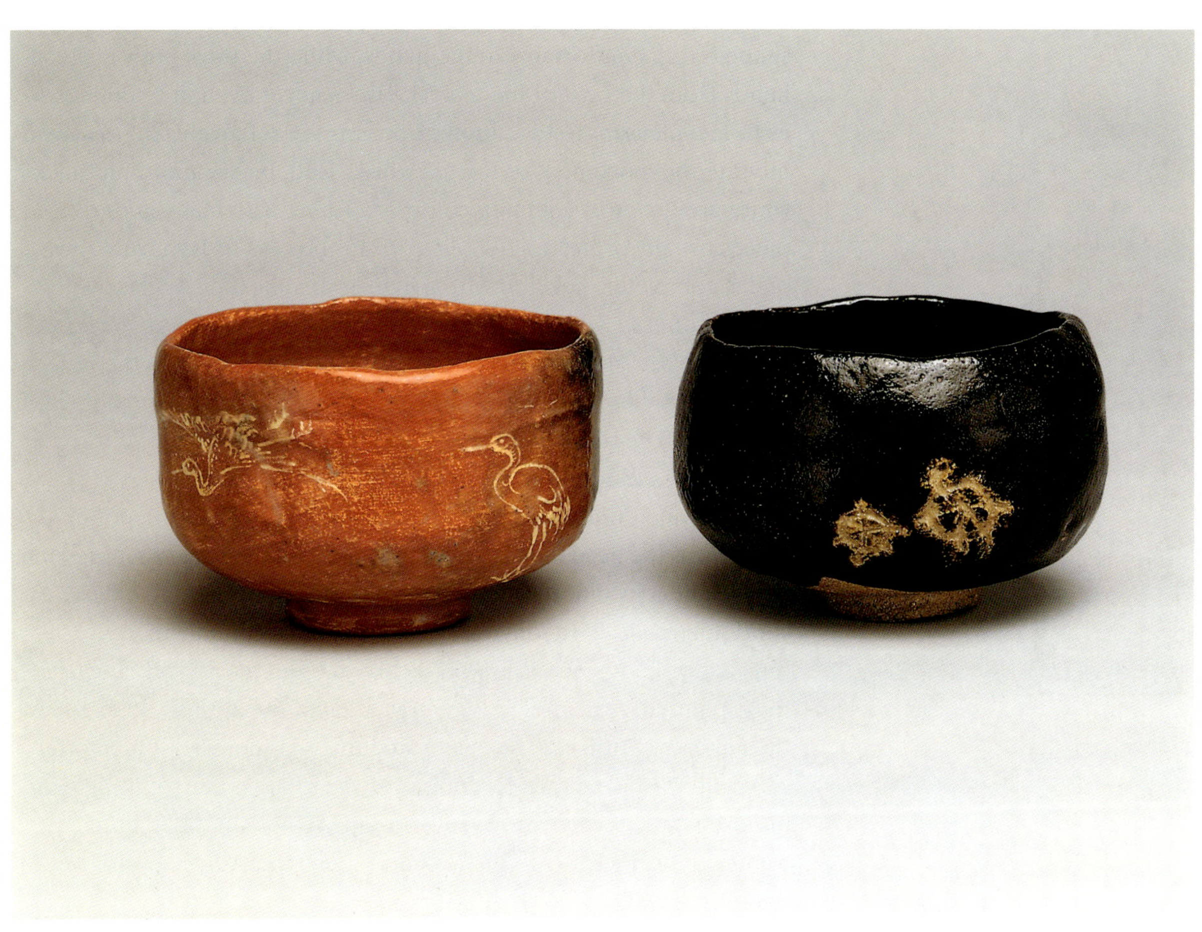

Plate 18 / No. 32
Two tea bowls
by Ryōnyū (1756–1834)
Raku ware
Seal: (each bowl) Raku
Edo period, late 18th–early 19th century
H: (red bowl) 8.1 cm, Diam: 12.2 cm
H: (black bowl) 8.1 cm, Diam: 11 cm

"commoner's tea," and Omote Senke, the way of the aristocrat—still function in Japan today.

It would be enlightening to describe the tea ceremony in its entirety and to discuss its many facets and influences upon art and culture. However, our main interest lies in its effect upon the development of ceramics, in particular the types of stoneware represented in this exhibition. Two Raku-ware tea bowls (Plate 18/No. 32) by Ryōnyū (1756–1834) have been chosen for discussion as they exemplify the type of ceramic traditionally prized by tea masters.

Raku ware was first produced in the late sixteenth century, possibly by a tilemaker named Chōjirō, the son of a Korean immigrant. The bowls, made from soft porous clay, are never perfectly round in shape but fit comfortably in the hands, while the thick body protects hands from the heat of the tea. The lip is never even; it undulates so as to feel pleasant to the mouth. Bottoms are relatively flat, to accommodate the movement of the tea whisk. Red, black, and sometimes white are the most common colors for Raku, with black-glazed pieces usually preferred for *chanoyu*. In the case of Ryōnyū's bowls, one is completely covered with a light-red, almost pink, glaze with touches of gray, while the other is black, except for the unglazed foot; both are impressed with the character for Raku. On the red bowl two cranes, one in flight and one standing, have been painted in white slip. The black bowl bears the scratched-out design of three small turtles. Both motifs are auspicious symbols.

Ryōnyū, at the age of fifteen, succeeded his father, the potter Chōnyū, as the head of his family. Having taken the name Kichizaemon, he became a prolific artist, working in both experimental and conventional modes. He sometimes decorated his ceramic pieces himself, although he occasionally turned them over to other artists to be painted. A man of varied interests and the author of a book on the genealogy of Raku, he celebrated the two-hundredth memorial service for his predecessor Chōjirō by creating and distributing two hundred "red bowls." In 1811 he became a monk but continued to pursue his interests in the tea ceremony, poetry, calligraphy, and painting.

Another object made for use in the tea ceremony is a water jar (Fig. 16/No. 36) by Takahara Shōji (b. 1941). The bucket-shaped flower container (Fig. 17/No. 37) by Suzuki Kōichi (b. 1942) could be employed to display a flower arrangement in the *tokonoma* of a tea room. Both are examples of Bizen ware, a type of pottery appreciated by the tea master Rikyū for its natural, earthy qualities. In contrast to the soft Raku ware, Bizen is a hard, reddish-brown stoneware, unglazed as a rule, but fired at such high temperatures that a natural glaze, formed by kiln ash, or streaks from rice-straw wrappings, appears on the surface in irregular patches. In earlier times, accidental flaws in Bizen ware, caused by the heat of the kiln or mishandling of pots prior to firing, appealed to the aesthetic sense of tea masters.

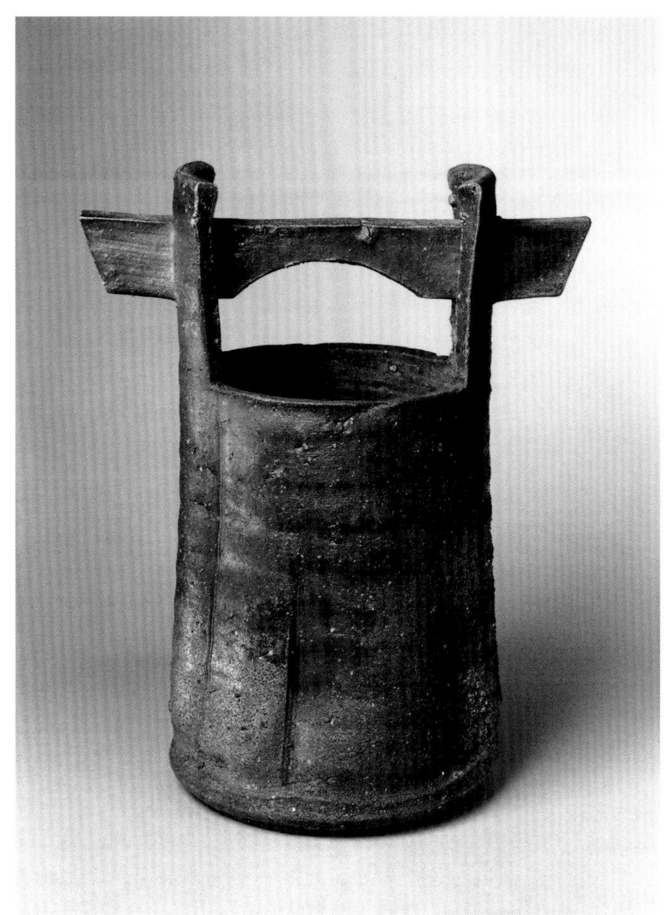

Fig. 17 / No. 37
Flower container in the shape of a bucket
by Suzuki Kōichi (b. 1942)
Bizen ware
20th century
H: 26.1 cm, Diam: 20.5 cm

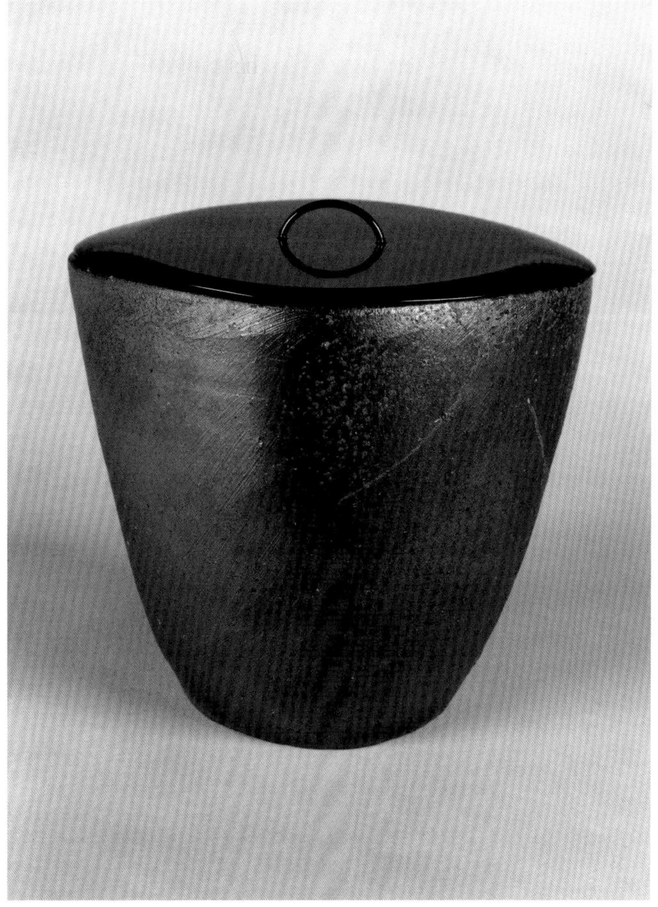

Fig. 16 / No. 36
Water jar
by Takahara Shōji (b. 1941)
Bizen ware
20th century
H: 16.6 cm, Diam: 19.1 cm

These two pieces are symmetrical, but many contemporary Bizen wares are intentionally designed with flawed or irregular shapes.

While rough stonewares were favored by later tea masters, ceramic artists also produced delicate, colorful porcelain pieces. Porcelain clay, known to the Chinese as early as the seventh century, was first found in Japan in the 1600s, and production of porcelain wares may have begun as early as 1610. Two small Edo-period dishes exhibited here are charming reflections of Japanese decorative taste. The dish with a design of pomegranates, peaches, and finger citron (Plate 19/No. 43) is an example of Kakiemon ware (also known as Kakiemon-style Arita ware); the dish with a design of fans and interlinking circles is Nabeshima ware (Plate 20/No. 46). Kakiemon ware is an overglaze-enameled porcelain known for its delicate, refined brushwork and clear colors—red, blue, yellow, black, and sometimes gold—sparingly applied to the creamy white ground. It features subjects which are usually Chinese in flavor, although European figures, flowers, and landscapes may also appear. Kakiemon-style ceramics were popular export wares, and included such objects as dishes, bowls, bottles, incense burners, flower vases, teapots, and teacups (Western style), and ornamental figures made specifically for Western trade. Tradition has it that the founder of Kakiemon ware was the potter Kizaemon (1596–1666), renamed by his overlord in appreciation of a porcelain ornament he had made in the shape of a persimmon *(kaki)*.

Nabeshima ware was produced at the official kiln of the Nabeshima *daimyō* in what is now Saga Prefecture, Kyūshū. The kiln opened in 1677, and its porcelains were not made for the export market but were designed to appeal to native taste. Nabeshima wares were made for use by the *daimyō*, and as gifts to the shogunate and imperial court. Most were shallow dishes, with underglaze-blue exteriors and a high foot decorated with a comb pattern. Their designs, elegant and precisely executed in underglaze blue and overglaze polychrome, are among the most varied, striking, and inventive to be found among Japanese porcelains. They sometimes feature elements of textile patterns, as can be seen on the example reproduced here. This composition consists of fans placed against a background of celadon and a design of interlinking circles in blue; the overall effect is one of abstract design rather than representational image.

An increase in porcelain production during the late seventeenth and eighteenth centuries was in part a response to the demands of Dutch merchants. Full-scale purchase of Japanese ceramics by the Dutch East India Company began as early as 1659. During this period of trade, production techniques improved and stylistic changes occurred in the decoration of pieces intended for export. Many porcelains were made to reflect Dutch taste and needs. One example of such a piece is the seventeenth-century Arita-ware ewer in this exhibition (No. 38). Its underglaze blue design consists of medallions containing abbreviated landscapes, with scrolling floral motifs between them and on the neck of the vessel. The main pictorial elements—mountains, a country pavilion, figures with parasols, and birds—are typical of Arita-ware export pieces.

Two examples of porcelain are of interest because of their connection with the Dutch. Both are decorated with figures of exotic foreigners and were probably made not for export but for the delight of the Japanese. The eighteenth-century four-sided *sake* bottle (Plate 21/No. 42) with a design of Dutchmen is an Arita-ware piece that may have been made for home use. It features four amusing depictions of the foreigners; two sides depict a trader with a dog, the other two, a trader smoking a pipe. The interior of the Imari-ware *Five Ships Bowl* (No. 47) is decorated with three ships bearing foreigners, and eight large figures of red-haired Dutchmen set against a crest-like pattern. Two additional ships and a peony design grace the exterior.

Both of these objects bring to mind the question so often asked of me: "What made you start to collect Japanese art?" Perhaps they also help me to answer that question. Ceramics and other objects depicting foreign themes or Dutch traders must have been viewed by the Japanese as highly exotic souvenirs. When I think back to my initial encounter with Japanese art, I realize that it is an infatuation with the foreign that often sets the collector on his quest. Upon seeing Japanese prints, screens, and sculptures, I asked myself: what motivated these people who seem so different from me? If I purchase this mysterious, decorative object (my first Genji screen, Plate 3/No. 26), will I understand them? The answer, of course, is no, but with genuine curiosity and luck, it is possible to go beyond the mere accumulation of curious and appealing "souvenirs" and acquire not only knowledge of the art of another culture but also a deeper understanding of that culture. Equally important to me are the insights I have gained into what such art means to people of my own culture. Thus, in spite of all of the work entailed in preparing any exhibition, the preparation involved for this one has been a truly rewarding experience.

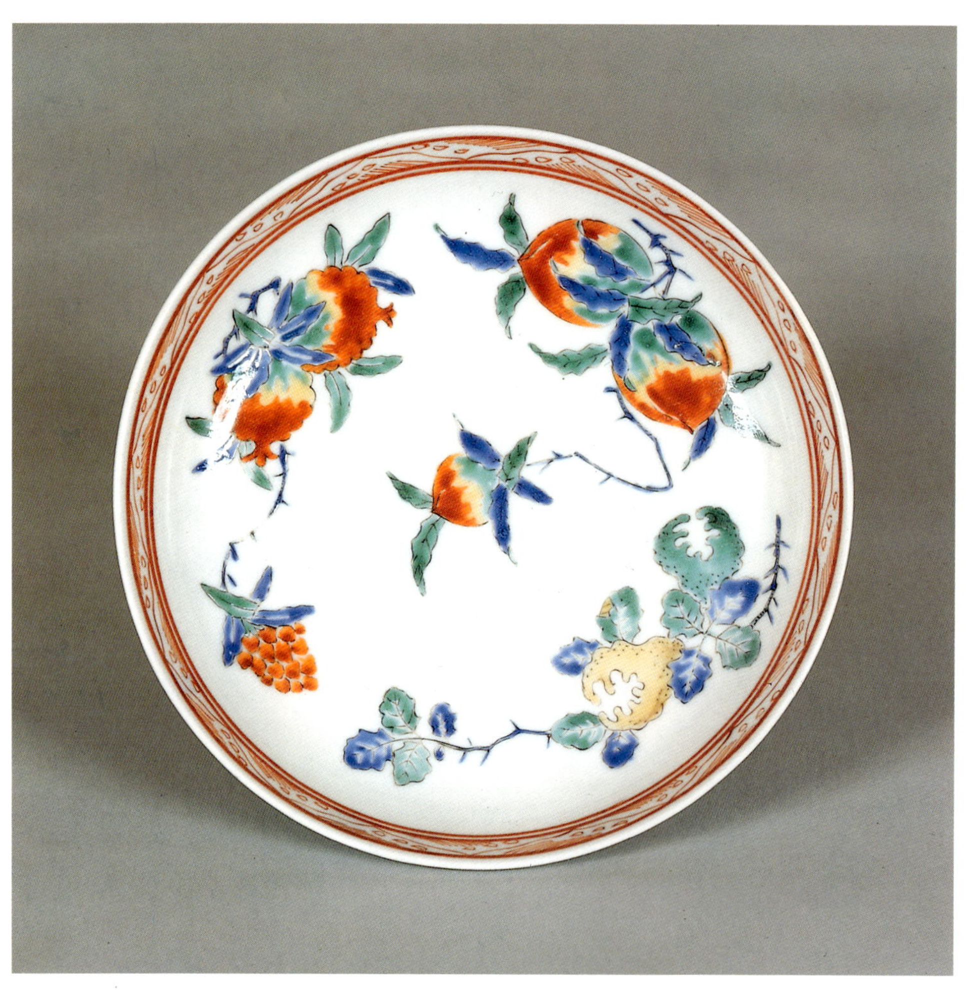

Plate 19 / No. 43
Dish with design of pomegranates, peaches, and finger citron
Kakiemon ware
painting in overglaze enamels
Edo period, 18th century
H: 3 cm, Diam: 14.1 cm

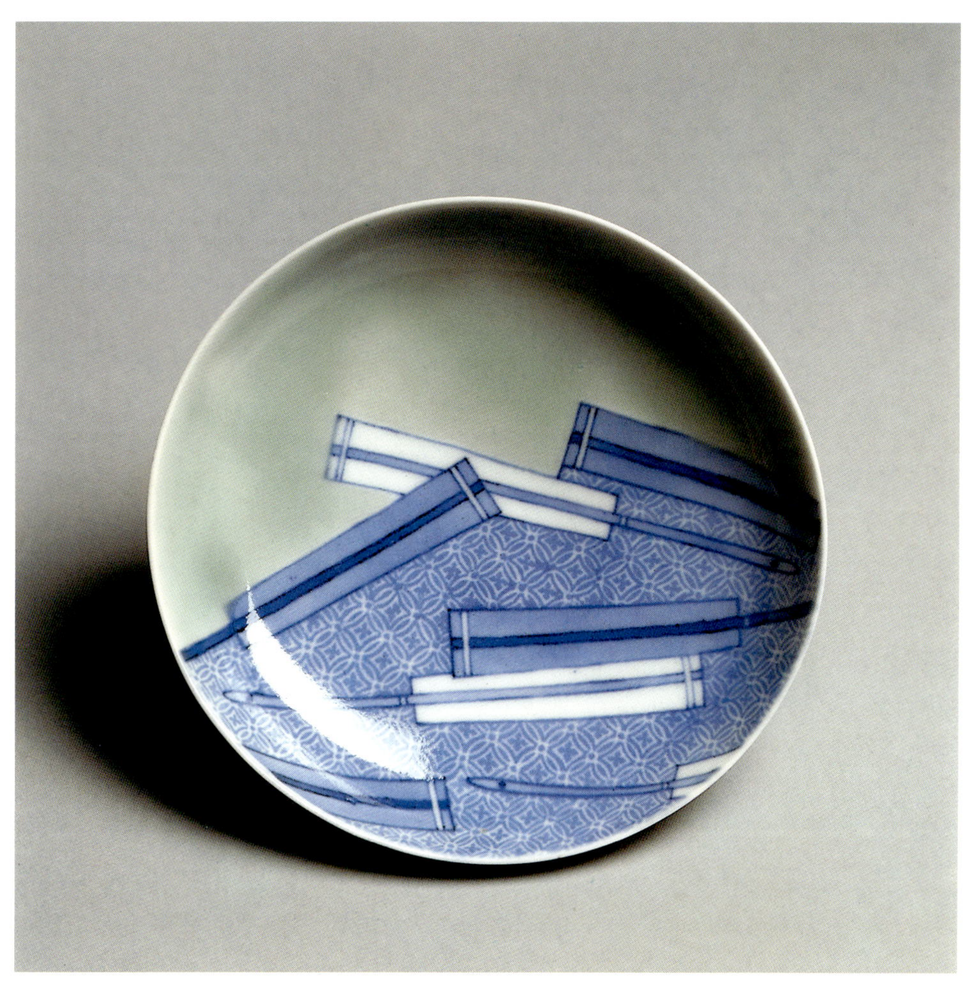

Plate 20 / No. 46
Dish with design of fans and interlinking circles
Nabeshima ware
celadon glaze with painting in underglaze blue
Edo period, 17th–19th century
H: 4.5 cm, Diam: 15.3 cm

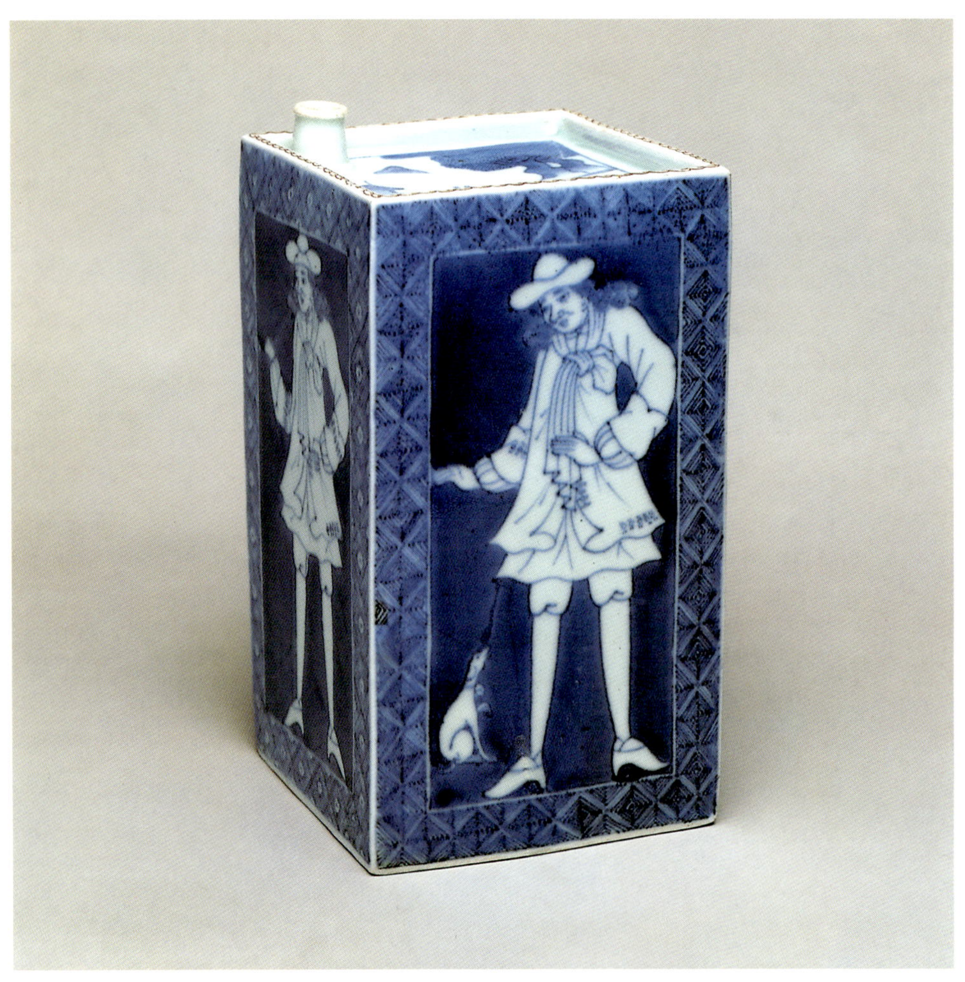

Plate 21 / No. 42
Sake bottle with
design of Dutchmen
Arita ware
painting in underglaze blue
Edo period, 18th century
H: 20.7 cm, Diam: 11.2 cm

CATALOGUE

Painting/Hanging scrolls

1/Fig. 2
Portrait of Rigen Daishi*
hanging scroll; color and ink on silk
Muromachi period, 16th century
90.5 x 41.9 cm

2/Plate 1
Kasuga Deer Mandala*
hanging scroll; color and ink
on paper
late Muromachi period to early
Edo period, 16th–17th century
89.9 x 40.0 cm

3/Fig. 10
Chrysanthemums
attributed to Tawaraya Sōsetsu
(fl. 1639–1650)
Seal: Inen
hanging scroll; ink, light color,
and gold on paper
Edo period, 17th century
123.9 x 49.8 cm

4/Plate 5
The Bodhisattva Monju*
by Kiyohara Yukinobu (1643–1682)
Signature: Kiyohara-shi no musume
Yukinobu hitsu
Seal: Kiyohara-jo
hanging scroll; color, ink, and
gold on silk
Edo period, 17th century
62.4 x 36.0 cm

5/Fig. 11
"Utsu no yama" episode from
Chapter 9 of *The Tales of Ise*
attributed to Fukae Roshū
(1699–1757)
hanging scroll; color and ink
on paper
Edo period, 18th century
22.2 x 46.2 cm

* The property of The Mary and Jackson Burke Foundation. All other objects are the property of The Mary and Jackson Burke Collection. (For dimensions of paintings and screens, height precedes width.)

6
A parody on the Third Princess and
Her Cat, from Chapter 35 of
*The Tale of Genji**
attributed to Matsuno Chikanobu
(fl. 1716–1735)
hanging scroll; color and ink
on paper
Edo period, 18th century
79.9 x 29.6 cm

7/Fig. 8
Dream of the New Year
by Hakuin (1685–1768)
Cipher: Hakuin
Seals: Ryūtoku Senten, Hakuin,
Ekaku-no-in
hanging scroll; ink on paper
Edo period, 18th century
52.0 x 64.6 cm

8/Fig. 12
The Four Accomplishments
by Ike Taiga (1723–1776)
Signature: Kashō
Seals: Sekitei, Ike Mumei in
hanging scroll; ink on paper
Edo period, 18th century
56.6 x 124.3 cm

9
Bird on a Branch
attributed to Nagasawa Rōsetsu
(1754–1799)
Signature: Rōsetsu
Seal: Gyo
hanging scroll; ink and light color
on paper
Edo period, 18th century
126.6 x 45.8 cm

10/Fig. 15
Chinese Officials and Scholars
with Attendants*
attributed to Nagasawa Rōsetsu
(1754–1799)
Signature: Rōsetsu
Seal: Gyo
hanging scroll; ink and light
color on paper
Edo period, 18th century
131.1 x 60.1 cm

11/Plate 11
Dutch Lady with Attendant
hanging scroll; color and ink on silk
Edo period, late 18th century
106.5 x 34.5 cm

12
Narcissus
by Nakamura Hōchū
(fl. late 18th–early 19th century)
Signature: Hōchū
Seal: illegible
hanging scroll; ink, color,
and gold on paper
Edo period, 19th century
20.7 x 17.3 cm

13
Calabash Vine with Insect*
by Maruyama Ōshin (1790–1838)
Signature: Ōshin
Seal: Ōshin-no-in
hanging scroll; color, and gold
on silk
Edo period, 19th century
99.8 x 36.4 cm

14/Plate 7
Hollyhocks and Lilies
by Suzuki Kiitsu (1796–1858)
Signature: Seisei Kiitsu
Seal: Shukurin
hanging scroll; ink, color, and
gold on silk
Edo period, 19th century
110.0 x 35.0 cm

15/Fig. 13
Travelers in Cold Mountains
by Hine Taizan (1813–1869)
Signature: Shibi [1859]
fuyu jūichi gatsu
Taizan rōjō ni utsusu hi shōnen
Seals: Sansei ji taiko,
Hi Chōjo Shōnen
hanging scroll; ink and light
color on silk
Edo period, 19th century
137.2 x 51.5 cm

16
Fireworks at Ryōgoku on the
Sumida River*
by Utagawa Hiroshige II (1826–1869)
Seal: Ryūsai
hanging scroll; color and ink on silk
Edo period, 19th century
98.4 x 33.8 cm

17/Plate 10 (Frontispiece)
Cranes
by Watanabe Shōka (1835–1887)
Signature: Shōka kore o egaku
Seals: Kai-no-in, Shōka
hanging scroll; color and ink on silk
Edo-Meiji period, 19th century
89.6 x 34.5 cm

18/Plates 12, 13
Amanoiwato and The Death of
Śākyamuni Buddha*
by Kōno Bairei (1844–1895)
Seal: (each painting) Kōno hōin
pair of hanging scrolls; ink, color,
and gold on silk
Meiji period, 19th century
70.5 x 27.0 cm (each scroll)

Painting/Albums and Handscrolls

19/Fig. 7 (detail)
"Aoi" episode from
Chapter 9 of *The Tale of Genji**
handscroll; ink on paper
Muromachi period, 16th century
12.0 x 572.0 cm

20/Plate 2 (detail), Fig. 3
Thirty-six Immortal Poetesses
album with 36 leaves; ink, color,
and gold on silk
Edo period, 17th century
Ptg. 6.1 x 9.8 cm (each leaf)
Call. 6.3 x 10.1 cm (each leaf)

21/Fig. 9
Eight Views of the Hsiao and
Hsiang Rivers
by Kano Tan'yū (1602–1674)
Seal: Tan'yū
album with 8 leaves; ink on silk
(Continued on next page)

Painting/Albums and Handscrolls

Edo period, 17th century
Ptg. 17.8 x 17.4 cm (each leaf)
Call. 19.5 x 18.5 cm (each leaf)

22/Fig. 6
Scenes from *The Tale of Genji**
album with 20 leaves; ink, color, and gold on paper
Edo period, 17th century
16.4 x 21.7 cm (each leaf)

23/Plate 9 (detail)
Scenes from the Yoshiwara District*
attributed to Ō'oka Michinobu (fl. 1720–1740)
handscroll; ink, color, and gold on paper
Edo period, 18th century
29.2 x 660.0 cm

24/Plate 4 (detail)
Night Parade of One Hundred Demons
handscroll; ink and color on paper
Edo period, 19th century
23.2 x 488.4 cm

Screens

25/Plate 6
Islands and Pines
School of Sōtatsu
Signature: (each screen) Sōtatsu Hokkyō
Seal: (each screen) Taisei-ken
pair of six-fold screens; ink, color, and gold on paper
Edo period, 17th century
154.5 x 357.8 cm (each screen)

26/Plate 3
Scenes from *The Tale of Genji*
six-fold screen; ink, color, and gold on paper
Edo period, 18th century
153.8 x 358.2 cm

27/Plate 8 (detail)
Two Beauties
by Tsukioka Settei (1710–1786)
Signature: (each panel) Hokkyō Tsukioka Settei tawamure ni egaku
Seal: (each panel) Hokkyō Settei
two-fold screen; ink and color on silk
Edo period, 18th century
114.3 x 41.9 cm (each panel)

28/Fig. 14
Goose and Reeds;
Willows and Moon
by Maruyama Ōkyo (1733–1795)
Signature: (left screen) Kichū [1793] chūshū ni utsusu Ōkyo; (right screen) An-ei Kōgo [1774] kito ni utsusu Ōkyo
Seal: (left screen) Ōkyo-no-in; (right screen) Ōkyo-no-in, Chūsen
pair of six-fold screens; ink, light color, and gold wash on paper
Edo period, 18th century
153.9 x 354.2 cm (left screen);
153.9 x 353.8 cm (right screen)

Sculpture

29/Fig. 1
Sōgyō Hachiman
wood with traces of pigment
Heian period, 12th century(?)
H: 34.3 cm

Ceramics/Stoneware

30
Storage jar
Tokoname ware(?)
Edo period, 17th century
H: 56 cm, Diam: 42.2 cm

31
Storage jar
Tamba ware(?)
Edo period, 17th century
H: 40.3 cm, Diam: 33.5 cm

32/Plate 18
Two tea bowls
by Ryōnyū (1756–1834)
Raku ware
Seal: (each bowl) Raku
Edo period, late 18th–
early 19th century
H: (red bowl) 8.1 cm, Diam: 12.2 cm
H: (black bowl) 8.1 cm, Diam: 11 cm

33
Jar with design of *murasaki* plant
by Takeda Toshio (b. 1932)
20th century
H: 26.7 cm, Diam: 38 cm

34
Flower container
by Kishimoto Kennin (b. 1934)
Iga ware
20th century
H: 34 cm, W: 21.6 cm

35
Covered box with design of
pampas grass
by Fukukawa Toshiko (b. 1939)
20th century
H: 10.1 cm, L: 19.5 cm, W: 19.2 cm

36/Fig. 16
Water jar
by Takahara Shōji (b. 1941)
Bizen ware
20th century
H: 16.6 cm, Diam: 19.1 cm

37/Fig. 17
Flower container in the shape
of a bucket
by Suzuki Kōichi (b. 1942)
Bizen ware
20th century
H: 26.1 cm, Diam: 20.5 cm

Ceramics/Porcelain

38
Ewer with landscape and
floral design
Arita ware
painting in underglaze blue
Edo period, 17th century
H: 28.2 cm, Diam: 16.6 cm

39
Plate with design of a bird
on a branch
Ko-Kutani ware
painting in overglaze enamels
Edo period, 17th century
H: 2.8 cm, Diam: 14.6 cm

40
Sake bottle with paulownia design
Kiyomizu ware
painting in underglaze iron brown
Edo period, 17th century
H: 15.6 cm, Diam: 12.8 cm

41
Covered jar with design of
chrysanthemum and *fujibakama*
plant
Hirado ware
painting in underglaze blue
Edo period, 18th century
H: 14.9 cm, Diam: 15.3 cm

42/Plate 21
Sake bottle with design of
Dutchmen*
Arita ware
painting in underglaze blue
Edo period, 18th century
H: 20.7 cm, Diam: 11.2 cm

43/Plate 19
Dish with design of pomegranates,
peaches, and finger citron
Kakiemon ware
painting in overglaze enamels
Edo period, 18th century
H: 3 cm, Diam: 14.1 cm

44
Dish with peony design*
Nabeshima ware
painting in underglaze blue
Edo period, 18th century
H: 4 cm, Diam: 14.5 cm

45
Dish
Nabeshima ware
celadon glaze with underglaze
blue rim
Edo period, 17th–19th century
H: 5.6 cm, Diam: 19.8 cm

46/Plate 20
Dish with design of fans and
interlinking circles
Nabeshima ware
celadon glaze with painting in
underglaze blue
Edo period, 17th–19th century
H: 4.5 cm, Diam: 15.3 cm

47
Five Ships Bowl
Imari ware
painting in overglaze enamels
Edo period, 18th–19th century
H: 14.2 cm, Diam: 30 cm

Lacquer

48
Cabinet with grapevine design*
black lacquer with sprinkled gold
Edo period, 17th century
H: 19.1 cm, L: 30.2 cm, W: 16 cm

49
Lobed incense burner with
cherry blossom design*
black lacquer with sprinkled gold
Edo period, 17th–18th century
H: 7.4 cm, Diam: 10 cm

50/Plate 14
Writing box with design of
bridge and waves
black lacquer with sprinkled gold,
metal and shell inlay
Edo period, 18th century
H: 4.3 cm, L: 22.4 cm, W: 21.0 cm

51
Gourd with lacquer design of
grapevine
by Hara Yōyūsai (1772–1845)
Signature: Yōyūsai
Edo period, 19th century
H: 18.1 cm, Diam: 9 cm

52/Fig. 4, Fig. 5 (detail)
Stacked boxes with design of the
Thirty-six Immortal Poets
black lacquer incised and colored
with gold
19th century
H: 45 cm, L: 25.9 cm, W: 24.4 cm

53/Plate 15
Zodiac calendar with holder in the
shape of a hanging scroll*
by Shibata Zeshin (1807–1891)
Signature: Kōka san [1846]
natsu hi sei reiya ta Zeshin
Seal: Koma
wood with lacquer, shell, and
sprinkled gold and silver
19th century
H: 25.7 cm, L: 7.8 cm, W: 4.3 cm
(holder)
L: 19.9 cm, W: 6.2 cm
(each plaque)

54/Plate 16
Tea caddy with "Autumn Fire
Design"
by Suzuki Mutsumi (b. 1941) and
Suzuki Misako (b. 1945)
black and red lacquer with
sprinkled gold
20th century
H: 7.7 cm, Diam: 7.2 cm

55/Plate 17
Tea caddy with "Cloud Design"
by Suzuki Mutsumi (b. 1941) and
Suzuki Misako (b. 1945)
red lacquer with
sprinkled gold and silver
20th century
H: 7.8 cm, Diam: 7.3 cm

BIBLIOGRAPHY

Books:

Addiss, Stephen. *Zenga and Nanga: Paintings by Japanese Monks and Scholars.* New Orleans: New Orleans Art Museum, 1976.

Addiss, Stephen et al. *A Myriad of Autumn Leaves: Japanese Art from the Kurt and Millie Gitter Collection.* New Orleans: New Orleans Museum of Art, 1984.

Akiyama Terukazu. *Japanese Painting.* Geneva: Editions d'Art Albert Skira, 1961.

Avitabile, Gunhild, ed. *Die Kunst des Alten Japan: Meisterwerke aus der Mary and Jackson Burke Collection, New York.* Frankfurt: Schirn Kunsthalle Frankfurt Am Römerberg/Kulturgesellschaft Frankfurt, 1990.

Awakawa Yasuichi. *Zen Painting.* Translated by John Bester. London: Kodansha International Ltd., 1970.

Baekeland, Frederick. *Imperial Japan: The Art of the Meiji Era (1868–1912).* New York: Cornell University, 1980.

Cahill, James. *Scholar Painters of Japan: The Nanga School.* New York: The Asia Society, 1972.

Daigoji no Mikkyō Bijutsu. Kyoto: 1975.

de Bary, William Theodore, ed. *Sources of Japanese Tradition.* New York: Columbia University Press, 1958.

Fontein, Jan, and Hickman, Money. *Zen Painting and Calligraphy.* Boston: The Museum of Fine Arts, 1970.

Freer Gallery of Art II: Japan. Tokyo: Kodansha Ltd., 1972.

Goff, Janet Emily. *Noh Drama and the Tale of Genji: The Art of Allusion in Fifteen Classical Plays.* Princeton: Princeton University Press, 1991.

Gorham, Hazel H. *Japanese and Oriental Ceramics.* Rutland, Vermont, and Tokyo: Charles Tuttle, 1971.

Impey, Oliver R. *The Lacquer of Suzuki Mutsumi and Suzuki Misako.* Oxford: The Ashmolean Museum, 1988.

Kageyama Haruki, and Kanda, Christine Guth. *Shinto Arts: Nature, Gods and Man in Japanese Art.* New York: Japan Society, 1976.

Kanazawa Hiroshi. *Japanese Ink Painting: Early Zen Masterpieces.* Translated by Barbara Ford. Tokyo: Kodansha Ltd. 1979.

Kanda, Christine Guth. *Shinzō: Hachiman Imagery and Its Development.* Cambridge, Mass.: Harvard University Press, 1985.

Kitabatake Chikafusa. *A Chronicle of Gods and Sovereigns: Jinnō Shōtōki.* Translated by H. Paul Varley. New York: Columbia University Press, 1980.

Kitagawa, Joseph M. *On Understanding Japanese Religion.* Princeton: Princeton University Press, 1987.

Kobayashi Tadashi, and Sakakibara Satoru. *Morikage and Itchō.* Nihon Bijutsu Kaiga Zenshū, vol. 16. Tokyo: Shueisha, 1978.

The Kodansha Encyclopedia of Japan. 9 vols. Tokyo: Kodansha Ltd., 1983.

Koji Kotowaza Jiten. Tokyo: Ōbunsha, 1983.

Kojiki. Translated with an introduction and notes by Donald L. Philippi. Princeton: Princeton University Press, 1969.

Lee, Sherman. *Japanese Decorative Style.* Cleveland: The Cleveland Museum of Art, 1961.

Link, Howard A., and Shimbo Tōru. *Exquisite Visions: Rimpa Paintings from Japan.* Tokyo: Gakken Publishing Co., 1980.

Masterpieces from the Shin'enkan Collection: Japanese Painting of the Edo Period. Los Angeles: Los Angeles County Museum of Art, 1986.

McCullough, Helen Craig. *Tales of Ise: Lyric Episodes from Tenth Century Japan.* Stanford: Stanford University Press, 1968.

Meech-Pekarik, Julia. *The World of the Meiji Print: Impressions of a New Civilization.* New York and Tokyo: Weatherhill, 1986.

Mino Yutaka et al. *The Great Eastern Temple: Treasures of Japanese Buddhist Art from Tōdai-ji.* Chicago: The Art Institute, 1986.

Mody, N.H.N. *A Collection of Nagasaki Colour Prints and Paintings Showing the Influence of Chinese and European Art on that of Japan.* Rutland, Vermont, and Tokyo: Charles Tuttle, 1969.

Munroe, Alexandra, and Richard, Naomi Noble, eds. *The Burghley Porcelains.* New York: The Japan Society, 1988.

Murase Miyeko. *Court and Samurai in an Age of Transition: Medieval Paintings and Blades from the Gotoh Museum.* New York: Japan Society, 1990.

__________ . *Japanese Art: Selections from the Mary and Jackson Burke Collection.* New York: The Metropolitan Museum of Art, 1975.

__________. *The Tale of Genji: Genji Monogatari Ekotoba.* New York and Tokyo: Weatherhill, 1983.

__________. *Tales of Japan: Scrolls and Prints from the New York Public Library.* New York and Oxford: Oxford University Press, 1986.

__________. *Urban Beauties and Rural Charms: Japanese Art from the Mary and Jackson Burke Foundation.* Orlando: Loch Haven Art Center, 1980.

Ōkyo and the Maruyama-Shijō School of Japanese Painting. St. Louis: The St. Louis Art Museum, 1980.

Pearson, Richard. *Ancient Japan.* Washington, D.C.: The Smithsonian Institution, 1992.

Pekarik, Andrew J. *Japanese Lacquer, 1600–1900: Selections from the Charles A. Greenfield Collection.* New York: The Metropolitan Museum of Art, 1980.

__________. *The Thirty-six Immortal Women Poets: A Poetry Album with Illustrations by Chōbunsai Eishi.* New York: George Braziller, Inc., 1991.

Piepenburg, Robert. *Raku Pottery.* New York: Macmillan, 1972.

Roberts, Laurance. *A Dictionary of Japanese Artists.* New York and Tokyo: Weatherhill, 1976.

Rosenfield, John M., and ten Grotenhuis, Elizabeth. *Journey of the Three Jewels: Japanese Buddhist Painting from Western Collections.* New York: The Asia Society and John Weatherhill, Inc., 1979.

Sawa Ryūken. *Mikkyō Jiten.* Kyoto: 1975.

Shimizu Yoshiaki. *Japan: The Shaping of Daimyo Culture, 1185–1868.* Washington, D.C.: National Gallery of Art, 1988.

Stevens, John, with Yelen, Alice Rae. *Zenga: Brushstrokes of Enlightenment.* New Orleans: New Orleans Museum of Art, 1990.

Tanaka Ichimatsu. *Japanese Ink Painting: Shubun to Sesson.* Translated by Bruce Darling. New York and Tokyo: Weatherhill/Heibonsha, 1972.

Tanizaki Jun'ichirō. *In Praise of Shadows.* Translated by Thomas J. Harper and Edward G. Seidensticker. New Haven: Leete's Island Books, 1977.

Varley, H. Paul. *Japanese Culture.* 3rd edition. Honolulu: The University of Hawaii Press, 1984.

Watt, James C. Y., and Ford, Barbara Brennan. *East Asian Lacquer.* New York: The Metropolitan Museum of Art, 1992.

Werner, E.T.C. *A Dictionary of Chinese Mythology*. Shanghai: Kelly and Walsh, 1932.

Wheelwright, Carolyn Kell. *Kano Shōei*. 2 vols., Ph.D. dissertation. Ann Arbor: University Microfilms International, 1981.

Yamasaki Taiko. *Shingon: Japanese Esoteric Buddhism*. Boston and London: Shambhala, 1988.

Yonezawa Yoshiho, and Yoshizawa Chu. *Japanese Painting in the Literati Style*. New York and Tokyo: Weatherhill/Heibonsha, 1974.

Periodicals:

Addiss, Stephen. "Visions of Enlightenment: Japanese Zen Painting and Calligraphy." *Orientations* (Jan. 1989): 24–32.

Browne, Michael L. "Portraits of Foreigners by Kawahara Keiga." *Ars Orientalis*, Vol. 15 (1985): 31–37.

Burke, Mary. "Twisted Pine Branches: Recollections of a Collector." *Apollo* (Feb. 1985): 77–84.

Earle, Joe. "New Styles in Lacquer." *Connoisseur* (Aug. 1981): 315–317.

Kaufman, Laura. "Practice and Piety: Buddhist Art in Use." *Apollo* (Feb. 1985): 90–100.

Moran, Sherwood. "The Death of Buddha: A Painting at Kōyasan." *Artibus Asiae*, Vol. 36, 1/2 (1974): 97–147.

Murase Miyeko. "Themes from Three Romantic Narratives of the Heian Period." *Apollo* (Feb. 1985): 100–130.

Segraves, Julia. "The Lacquer Work of Suzuki Mitsumi." *Arts of Asia* (Sept.–Oct. 1987): 109–117.

Photograph Credits:

Sheldan Comfert Collins: Interior of tea room (page 4); Plates 1, 2 (endpiece), 5, 6, 20; Figs. 2, 4, 5, 14, 17

©Carl Nardiello: Plates 4, 7, 8, 9, 10 (frontispiece), 11, 12, 13, 14, 15, 16, 17, 18, 19, 21; Figs. 3, 6, 7, 9, 12, 15, 16; Page 70, detail of lacquer box No. 48

Otto E. Nelson: Figs. 1, 8, 10, 11, 13

©Malcolm Varon: Cover, Plate 3

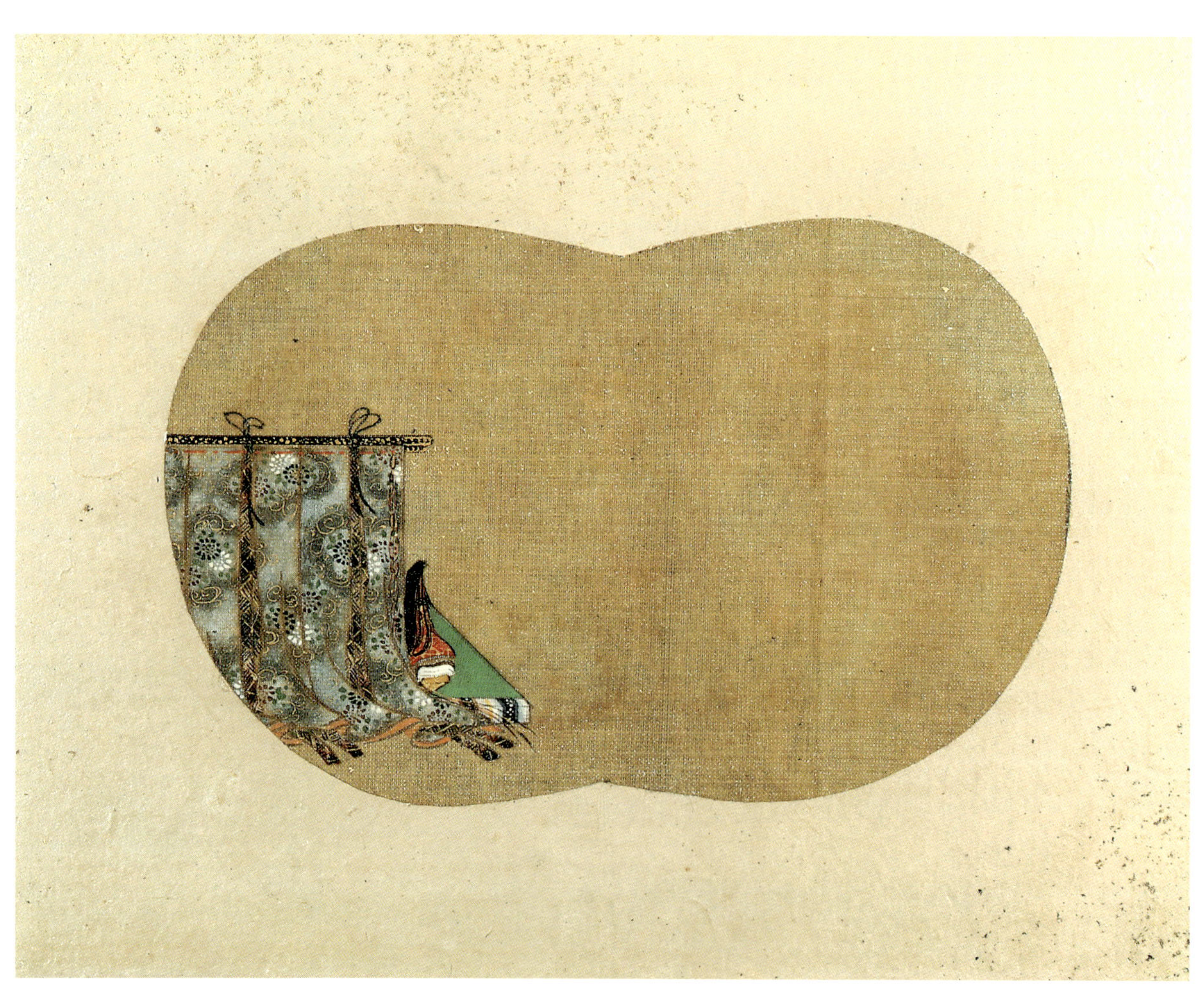

Plate 2 (detail) / No. 20
Thirty-six Immortal Poetesses
album with 36 leaves;
ink, color, and gold on silk
Edo period, 17th century
Ptg. 6.1 x 9.8 cm (each leaf)
Call. 6.3 x 10.1 cm (each leaf)